LUCY IN THE MIND OF LENNON

INNER LIVES

SERIES EDITOR
William Todd Schultz

———————

Dan P. McAdams
GEORGE W. BUSH

William Todd Schultz
TRUMAN CAPOTE

Tim Kasser
JOHN LENNON

LUCY IN THE MIND OF LENNON

Tim Kasser

OXFORD
UNIVERSITY PRESS

OXFORD
UNIVERSITY PRESS

Oxford University Press is a department of the University of Oxford.
It furthers the University's objective of excellence in research, scholarship,
and education by publishing worldwide.

Oxford   New York
Auckland   Cape Town   Dar es Salaam   Hong Kong   Karachi
Kuala Lumpur   Madrid   Melbourne   Mexico City   Nairobi
New Delhi   Shanghai   Taipei   Toronto

With offices in
Argentina   Austria   Brazil   Chile   Czech Republic   France   Greece
Guatemala   Hungary   Italy   Japan   Poland   Portugal   Singapore
South Korea   Switzerland   Thailand   Turkey   Ukraine   Vietnam

Oxford is a registered trademark of Oxford University Press in the UK and certain other
countries.

Published in the United States of America by
Oxford University Press
198 Madison Avenue, New York, NY 10016

© Oxford University Press 2013

Library of Congress Cataloging-in-Publication Data
Kasser, Tim.
Lucy in the mind of Lennon / Tim Kasser.
    p. cm.—(Inner lives)
Includes bibliographical references and index.
ISBN 978–0–19–974760–3
1. Lennon, John, 1940–1980. Lucy in the sky with diamonds.   2. Lennon, John,
1940–1980—Psychology.   I. Title.
ML420.L38K37 2013
782.42166092—dc23
2012037946

To my parents,
with thanks

Our LPs reflect where we are at the moment, and *Pepper* reflected the changes we were going through and what we looked forward to…that symbolism, however, only exists in people's minds—therefore it's right. If an intellectual sees intellectual shit in it, it's there. And if a drug addict sees drug shit in it, it's there.

Even some of the records I made, when you talk about them, at the time I wasn't consciously knowing what I'm doing, in a way. And it's only when you look back at it, you "Oh, I see what I was feeling at that time" (sic). Even though one tried to express it in the music, you're not conscious of what you're expressing….

I think everything comes out in the songs…It's just harder to see when it's written in gobbledygook.

—*John Lennon*

CONTENTS

PREFACE

I'm not one who reminisces much about my childhood, but I do have a vivid memory from the late 1970s of a friend handing me *The Beatles 1962–1966* and *The Beatles 1967–1970*. I remember looking at the covers of those red and blue albums and being amazed at the change in the physical appearance of each of the Beatles from the early to the late 1960s. I also remember a year or two later when I heard that John Lennon had been killed—I believe I was in the locker room of my high school gym. Perhaps because of the flood of Lennon's songs played on the radio in the aftermath of his murder, the Beatles soon became my favorite band and Lennon my favorite Beatle.

Once I became a psychology major in college, I began thinking about writing a biography about Lennon. I wondered how I could explain the various twists and turns of his life, or of any life for that matter. I started and stopped writing about Lennon several times over the next two decades. Looking back, I see that when I began those aborted projects, I was too much of a fan to look at Lennon with anything approaching objectivity. Those projects were set aside as I moved in the direction typical of most research psychologists, collecting surveys from and doing experiments on hundreds of study participants and analyzing the resulting data with increasingly sophisticated statistical techniques.

But I never lost my fascination with biography, with Lennon, or with attempts to understand a particular person. While these interests did not really influence my scholarly work, I have been able to express them in my teaching at Knox College. Classes like *Theories of Personality* and *Clinical and Abnormal Psychology* lend themselves quite well to discussions of specific individuals, and I have tried to take advantage of that fact. A class on *Dreaming* that I have taught a half dozen times has also let me get deeply inside people's minds by trying to understand the seemingly bizarre stories and images they create throughout the night. And in a class called *The Study of the Person*, my students and I have tried to understand how one can come close to understanding the life of a single individual. Indeed, the last few times I have taught that class, Lennon was one of the people whom we tried to understand together.

Through these discussions with my students, I came to understand a good deal more about Lennon and eventually lost my idealization of him. While I still feel that he was a courageous person and a remarkably inventive artist and social activist, I also came to see him as someone who could often be quite irresponsible and self-centered. Alan Elms, one of the leaders in the field of psychobiography, warns that biographers should neither love nor hate the people they are studying. Instead, the subject of a biography must be seen as what he or she actually was—a person with strengths and weaknesses, just like you and me. This attitude can be hard to maintain with someone as famous and complex as John Lennon. The range of Lennon's biographers—from fawning fans to those bent on tearing him down—prove this point well. I hope I follow neither of these models.

That said, this book is by no means an attempt to explain the whole of Lennon's life. Instead I hope to understand the particular time in this man's life when he was writing *Lucy in the Sky with Diamonds* in the early months of 1967. What was happening for Lennon in those moments? What was going on his mind? How did those moments relate to what had happened earlier in his life? And what, if anything, did this series of moments portend for the months that followed?

My attempts to answer these questions have been aided by a number of people. I must thank the many students who have taken my classes on *Dreaming* and *The Study of the Person*; working with them has helped me more than they probably know. Heather Hoffmann, Frank McAndrew, Daniel Peterson, and Kelly Shaw, my colleagues in the Psychology Department at Knox College, remain a source of ongoing support and information. Knox College itself has helped this project, both through its excellent library and by awarding me an Andrew W. Mellon Foundation Faculty Career Enhancement Grant. This helped pay the salaries of two research assistants, Lynda Joy Gerry and Kienan Crawford-Mackin, whose help I appreciate.

I also benefited from consultations with Brian Adams, David Bashwiner, Diana Beck, Sharon Clayton, Laura and Ron D'Angelo, Jaclyn Hennessey Ford, John Grow, John Haslem, Paul Marasa, Tony McCaffrey, Tom Moses, Tim Rairdon, Xavier Romano, Michael Schiano, Paul Siegel, Dean Simonton, and Roger Taylor. For their comments on drafts of individual chapters, I thank Cindy Chung, Jeremy Day-O'Connell, Amy Demorest, James Pennebaker, and three anonymous reviewers. For their comments on drafts of numerous chapters or of the entire book, I thank

Corrina Cordon, Paul Doughty, Shara Drew, David Gould, Mark Lerner, Maryjo McAndrew, Austin Mobley, and two anonymous reviewers.

I also especially thank Todd Schultz, the editor of this series on psychobiography, and Abby Gross, my editor at Oxford University Press, for their belief in this project and their very useful feedback.

And, as always, I am grateful to my wife Virginia for providing a patient sounding board for my ideas, a warm ear for my frustrations, clear editing of my writing, and all the happiness she brings me.

LUCY IN THE MIND OF LENNON

THE PROBLEM

When the Beatles released their album *Sgt. Pepper's Lonely Hearts Club Band* in the late spring of 1967, fans and critics alike were quick to find references to drugs throughout the LP. The album's deliriously decorated jacket featured marijuana plants in the garden behind which the Beatles stood. The lyrics of *With a Little Help from My Friends*, *Lovely Rita*, and *A Day in the Life* all referred to marijuana, mentioning getting "high" and taking "some tea," as well a desire to "turn you on." And tuned-in listeners easily connected the feelings, sensations, and visions people typically experience while on hallucinogenic drugs to the dreamlike imagery of *Lucy in the Sky with Diamonds*. Some clever listeners even pointed out that the song's title shares the initials of the hallucinogen LSD (lysergic acid diethylamide).

The Beatles had no doubt contributed to the perception that *Sgt. Pepper* was indeed a piece of hippie propaganda for hallucinogenic partying. Around the time the album was released, Paul McCartney revealed in a *Life* magazine interview that he had been using marijuana and LSD. McCartney even went on to extol the virtues of LSD, claiming that it had brought him closer to God and would yield world peace if only politicians would try it. Soon after, John Lennon, George Harrison, and the Beatles' manager Brian Epstein also admitted that they had used LSD. Later that summer, the Beatles endorsed the legalization of marijuana by signing their names to a full-page advertisement in the *London Times*.

Despite these public proclamations about his drug use, John Lennon steadfastly denied that *Lucy in the Sky with Diamonds* was about drugs. Even near the end of his life, when he was well protected from any negative consequences that might occur were he to admit the song's "true purpose," Lennon said:

> It was purely unconscious that it came out to be LSD. Until somebody pointed it out, I never even thought of it. I mean, who would ever bother to look at initials of a title? It's *not* an acid song (emphasis in original).

Lennon instead consistently claimed that the song was a response to a picture painted by his almost four-year-old son Julian. The oft-repeated story goes that Julian had brought the picture home from school and told his father that it was of his friend, Lucy, who was up in the sky with diamonds. Lennon's mind had then wandered toward the Lewis Carroll books *Alice in Wonderland* and *Through the Looking-Glass* that he had long admired and recently been re-reading. *Lucy in the Sky with Diamonds* was born when Lennon took images from Julian's picture and combined them with elements of Carroll's stories and poems.

A third explanation for the song's meaning and origin was provided by Lennon many years after it was written, just a few weeks before he was killed. While reflecting on each of the songs in his discography, Lennon said this about *Lucy in the Sky with Diamonds*:

> There was also the image of the female who would someday come save me—a "girl with kaleidoscope eyes" who would

come out of the sky. It turned out to be Yoko, though I hadn't met Yoko yet.... The imagery was Alice in the boat. And also the image of this female who would come and save me—this secret love that was going to come one day. So it turned out to be Yoko, though, and I hadn't met Yoko then. But she was my imaginary girl that we all have.

Lennon's 1980 explanation provided the springboard for yet another interpretation of the song. In a footnote to his 1994 book, *Revolution in the Head: The Beatles' Records and the Sixties*, music critic Ian MacDonald suggested the following:

The "girl with kaleidoscope eyes"...was, for Lennon, the lover/mother of his most helpless fantasies: "the image of the female who would someday come save me." This mysterious, oracular woman—mourned for in *Yes It Is* [Lennon's 1965 recording], bewildered by in *She Said, She Said* [Lennon's 1966 song]—was originally his mother, Julia, a role subsequently assumed by Yoko Ono [in the song *Julia*, Lennon's 1968 recording].

So here we have four explanations for the origin and meaning of *Lucy in the Sky with Diamonds*: (1) It is about the drug LSD; (2) it is a lyrical response to Julian's drawing, colored by the writings of Lewis Carroll; (3) it is about a female savior who turned out to be Yoko Ono; and (4) it is about Lennon's mother, Julia. Is only one of these explanations true? Are none of them true? Are they all true?

My sense is that while all of these explanations have some appeal, each one by itself is incomplete and only partially satisfying.

Consider the drug-based explanation. On the one hand, Lennon had clearly admitted that earlier songs of his were inspired by or referred to drugs. For example, only months after taking LSD for the first time, he recorded *Day Tripper*, poking fun at would-be hippies. *Tomorrow Never Knows* followed soon after, representing Lennon's attempts to aurally re-create the experience of tripping. Psychologically speaking, it is also quite plausible that Lennon's frequent ingestion of LSD could have made him unconsciously attracted to a picture whose title shared that acronym. Research studies show, for example, that people have strong but largely unconscious preferences for the letters of their own name, which can influence where they live (e.g., St. Louis has an over-representation of people named Louis) and the occupations they choose (e.g., dentists have an over-representation of people named Dennis). On the other hand, the initials LSD also stand for many other phrases and terms, including the British slang "Librae Solidi Denarii" (i.e., Pounds, Shillings, Pence), the Chicago street "Lake Shore Drive," the statistical test "Least Significant Difference," and the African bovine illness "Lumpy Skin Disease." As such, one might expect these initials to co-occur every now and again by chance in prolific songwriters. More importantly, it is clearly not the case that all people who take LSD experience the particular images and storyline that appear in *Lucy in the Sky with Diamonds*. Something more must have been active in Lennon's mind at the time he was composing the song.

Let us turn next to the explanation that the song was based on Julian's picture. Many people who knew Lennon have confirmed that such a picture exists and that it was the initial impetus for *Lucy in the Sky with Diamonds*. Lennon's first wife Cynthia, however, also wrote that Julian painted "endless pictures for Daddy." As far as we know, none of those other pictures inspired Lennon to write a song. What was special about this picture of Lucy? And while examination of Julian's picture confirms that it is of a girl floating in a sky among shapes that look like diamonds, there is little visible in the picture that suggests a direct association to Carroll's writings or to the plot line, specific images, and musical themes that eventually constituted the song Lennon wrote.

Compared to these rather superficial explanations of the song, Lennon's own 1980 explanation is certainly more complex and psychologically deep. However, one must keep in mind Lennon's well-known antagonism toward the clue hunters who searched for meaning in his lyrics. Consider, for example, his quote that opens this book, as well as Lennon's efforts in songs like *Glass Onion* to intentionally mislead listeners about the meanings of earlier songs (e.g., "The Walrus was Paul"). Had Lennon's attitude changed by 1980 so that he was now willing to reveal himself? Also problematic is that Lennon twice claimed in this same explanation that he had not yet met Yoko Ono before he wrote *Lucy in the Sky with Diamonds*, when, in fact, Lennon first met Yoko at an art gallery about three months before (in early November of 1966), had seen her again at an art opening in late November, received a copy of her book *Grapefruit* in the closing months of 1966, and even seems to have invited Yoko to lunch at his Kenwood home in January of 1967. While Lennon's memory for the chronology of events is unreliable for many other aspects of his life, one still must wonder why he would say that the song was about Yoko, but deny (twice) that he knew her when he wrote it.

And then we have Ian MacDonald's explanation. While it is an appropriate application of Sigmund Freud's theories about a boy's unresolved feelings toward his mother, MacDonald does little more to buttress his idea than to share a potentially interesting hunch and refer to three other songs Lennon wrote.

Given the array of potential explanations that have been provided for the meaning of *Lucy in the Sky with Diamonds*, and the limitations of each explanation, perhaps it is not surprising that Stephen Spignesi and Michael Lewis offered a fifth approach to the song in their book *Here, There, and Everywhere*:

> Is there an ultimate meaning to the song? Not empirically: The observation of the song's "reality" does not provide answers.

The problem with this statement is that, to my knowledge, an empirical observation of the song's reality has not yet been fully attempted. Previous explanations have provided rather superficial descriptions of the event that inspired the song's creation, unsubstantiated speculations about the role of drugs and women in its composition, and an introspective explanation by the song's author, who perhaps should not be fully trusted.

In this book, I therefore use psychological approaches to closely and systematically observe the song's "reality" so as to collect some empirical data that might shed light on the song's meaning, as well as on its place in Lennon's psyche. Typically psychologists ply their trade by giving people well-validated tests and interviews or by attaching their study participants to machines that measure physiological reactions, be it sweat on hands or firing of neurons in certain brain regions. Unfortunately, many of these standard strategies are not very practical—or even possible—for understanding a song written 45 years ago by a man who has been dead for more than 30 years. And even if he were still alive, I doubt that Lennon would cooperate much with such endeavors, given his rebellious personality and antipathy to such interpretations.

Nonetheless, a variety of tools, techniques, and rules for increasing the likelihood that some sense can be made of the events and products of a person's life are available, courtesy of psychologists interested in the study of individual lives, or what some call *psychobiography*. Two of these rules have already informed my analysis of Lennon's 1980 explanation for *Lucy in the Sky with Diamonds*: Irving Alexander warned psychobiographers to be particularly alert to (1) repeated denials (i.e., that Lennon had not met Yoko before the song was written) and (2) statements that are in error (i.e., Lennon had in fact met Yoko before composing the song). Both types of statements, according to Alexander, often suggest that something deeper may be occurring in the individual's mind.

Other tools developed by psychobiographers have been used to understand a variety of creative work, including short stories, letters, diaries, speeches, and even songs. These methods work by deeply analyzing the style, the content, and the storyline of such verbal creations, thereby illuminating certain psychological processes that may not be obvious to the naked eye of the observer. In the next four chapters, I use four such methods to closely examine the linguistic style, plot, words, and music of *Lucy in the Sky with Diamonds* so as to identify important characteristics of the song that might reveal something about Lennon's concerns at the time he was writing it. (Because this book does not reprint the lyrics or the music of *Lucy in the Sky with Diamonds*, readers may want to pull out their *Sgt. Pepper* album (or charge up their MP3 player) and give the song another listen. Readers who are particularly interested in the technical details and limitations of these methods may want to read the "Notes on the Methods" section of this book as they make their way through chapters 2 through 5).

Then, in chapter 6, I review and analyze biographical information about Lennon's childhood and adolescence, as well as the events in his life that preceded the composition of this song, so that in chapter 7 an integrative explanation can be provided for why Lennon composed *Lucy in the Sky with Diamonds* in the way he did during the winter of 1966–1967. Chapter 8 explores some of the songs Lennon recorded in the following months, showing how they tentatively continued to express the concerns that seem to have been behind *Lucy in the Sky with Diamonds*, at least until circumstances in Lennon's life shifted substantially. Finally, in chapter 9, I discuss how Lennon ultimately came to express these concerns explicitly, rather than in the highly opaque form that they took in *Lucy in the Sky with Diamonds*.

2 | THE STYLE

Here are brief excerpts from two poems about the end of a love affair. One of the poems was written by a woman who killed herself when she was 30, and the other by a woman who died of natural causes in her 70s. Which poet committed suicide? Was it Poet 1?

> The ache of marriage:
> We look for communion
> and are turned away, beloved,
> each and each…

Or Poet 2?

> I fancied you'd return the way you said,
> But I grow old and I forget your name…

The first poem was written by Denise Levertov, who lived into her 70s; the second was written by Sylvia Plath, who committed suicide at age 30. While both poems express remorse about the breakup, they are remarkably different in one seemingly small way: their use of first person singular pronouns. Plath, in talking about her pain, used the word "I" three times; in contrast, Levertov avoided the use of first person singular pronouns throughout the excerpt. This is important because, as it turns out, studies show that a consistent predictor of suicidality and depression (among both poets and non-poets) is the frequent use of first person singular pronouns, especially in the context of painful feelings. This aspect of the way a person speaks and writes seems to belie a tendency on the part of depressed (and suicidal) people to be overly aware of themselves and to strongly identify with their psychic pain; such tendencies probably both reflect and contribute to their depression. In contrast, nondepressed individuals seem able to distance themselves from such unpleasant feelings, and this psychologically adaptive tendency expresses itself in the way that such individuals write and speak.

Here's another question. During the investigation into the alleged kidnapping of two children, the distraught parents made the following statements to police. Which parent was later convicted of murdering the children? Was it Parent 1?

> "My children wanted me. They needed me. And now
> I can't help them."

Or Parent 2?

> "They're okay. They're going to be home soon."

The clue that helped police investigators identify the murdering parent is another seemingly small point of grammar, in this case, verb tense. Typically, when parents believe that their children are missing but alive, the children will be referred to in the present tense. This is how the children's father, David Smith, spoke of them in the second quote. But it seemed odd to the investigators that the mother, Susan Smith, spoke of her children in the past tense when she claimed that they had been kidnapped, and were therefore presumably only missing. In fact, her language expressed what she knew: Smith had strapped her two young sons into their car seats and sunk her automobile into a lake.

These examples suggest that people's *linguistic style*, or ways of using common words that find their way into most sentences, can actually reveal quite a bit about both their personalities and current situations. Said differently, people convey meaning not only by *what* they say, but *how* they say it. For example, like most children, I picked up on certain variations in linguistic style early in life, differentiating between when my mother or father called "Tim, please come to the kitchen" and "Timothy James Kasser, you get yourself to this kitchen right now." While in both cases the underlying message was identical (i.e., come to the kitchen), the two sentences conveyed clearly different meanings about the speaker's psychological state at that particular moment in time.

Research on people's linguistic style documents that word usage reflects both stable factors within people and the effects of particular situations in which they momentarily find themselves. For example, studies consistently show that older people are more likely than younger people to use more cognitively complex words (e.g., "cause," "wonder"), as well as more positive ("happy") and fewer negative ("angry") words to express emotion. Women are consistently more likely than men to talk about both positive and negative emotions and to express uncertainty (e.g., "maybe"). In contrast, men are more likely to use first person singular pronouns ("I") and adjectives reflecting a judgment (e.g., "bad"). As is the case with suicidal and depressed people, individuals with heightened *neuroticism* (or emotional instability) tend to refer to themselves with first person singular pronouns more often and to use more negative words to express emotion. Mortality is even predictable by the use of positive emotion words, as one study found the more that young nuns used positive words to express emotion in the short autobiographies they wrote when they took their vows, the more likely they were to be alive six or seven decades later.

While it is true that people's language can reflect aspects of their personalities that are stable from year to year, people also change their linguistic styles depending on their psychological situations. For example, research shows that the use of past tense verbs and hedging words (like "perhaps") varies depending on whether the person is addressing someone higher or lower in status. People also change their linguistic style when they are lying. One study compared people's language when they were asked to write down their true feelings about topics like abortion compared to when they were asked to lie about their attitudes toward those topics. Across a variety of topics, people who were lying decreased how often they used first person singular pronouns ("I," "me") and words signifying exclusion ("but," "without"), and increased the use of words conveying negative emotions ("angry") and motion ("go").

Shared social circumstances can also influence word usage. One study investigated linguistic styles in the blogs people wrote before and after the September 11, 2001 terrorist attacks on the United States. Compared to their linguistic styles before the attack, the days immediately after the attacks saw bloggers using fewer emotionally positive words, increasing their use of cognitive words ("because" and "understand"), and increasing their use of social words ("talk" and "friends"). These changes probably reflect the decrease in positive feelings people were experiencing, their desire to try to understand the attacks, and the tendency to reach out to others at a time of emotional upheaval, respectively. While all three of these indicators of linguistic style returned more or less to pre-9/11 levels within a couple of weeks, one change was still notable in the blogs six weeks later: People's language was significantly less "immediate," as they avoided the use of first person singular pronouns and of present tense verbs, presumably as a way to distance themselves from the here and now. Bloggers also remained high in their usage of big words (i.e., words with many letters), consistent with the possibility that they were "intellectualizing" in an attempt to avoid painful feelings.

The idea that linguistic style reflects both people's personalities and their current psychological states has been written about at great length by many psychologists over the decades. More contemporary psychological research on the topic (including much of what has just been reviewed) has benefited from a computer program developed by Dr. James Pennebaker at the University of Texas at Austin. This program, Linguistic Inquiry and Word Count (LIWC), quickly scans through a text of any length and searches out words that have been shown to be reliable indicators of around 70 preset categories. These categories include pronouns, verb tense, cognitive activity, and emotional words, but also prepositions (e.g., "over" and "under") and articles (e.g., "a" and "the"), words that concern space (e.g., "down") and time (e.g., "hour"), words that refer to discrepancies (e.g., "would" or "should"), and many others. Some words are classified by the LIWC computer program as simultaneously belonging to multiple categories. For example, words such as "laughed" would be classified as an "emotion," a "positive emotion," and a "past tense verb." After scanning through and categorizing a text, the LIWC program presents the user with information about the percentage of words that fall into each category.

The LIWC program has even been applied in the analysis of the linguistic styles of Beatles' songs. Pennebaker and his colleagues ran the LIWC program on the 85 songs written by John Lennon, the 67 by Paul McCartney, the 25 by George Harrison, and the 15 on which Lennon and McCartney collaborated extensively. (Ringo Starr's songs were omitted as he wrote so few while a member of the Beatles.) Quite a number of findings resulted from these analyses, but I will summarize two sets of results here.

First, the linguistic style of Beatles' songs changed substantially over the periods of 1960–1964, 1965–1967, and 1968–1970. As time went on, the Beatles used fewer sexual words (like "kiss"), fewer present tense and future tense verbs, and more words that were six letters or longer. One might say that these linguistic changes reflect maturation in the songwriters. That is, early on, when the Beatles were a pop band singing to throngs of screaming girls, *I Want to Hold Your Hand* was more their style. As they turned into a studio art-rock band, their work became more psychologically sophisticated, with songs like *Strawberry Fields Forever* and *The Fool on the Hill*.

The LIWC program also revealed that the linguistic styles of the composers differed in ways that are fairly consistent with common stereotypes about the personality of each Beatle. For example, Lennon used more negative emotional words across the 1960s than did his bandmates, confirming his angry and cynical image. Good examples include *I'll Cry Instead* ("I've got ev'ry reason on earth to be mad") and *Good Morning, Good Morning* (e.g., "feeling low down"). McCartney's romantic image is supported by the fact that he used first person plural words such as "we" and "us" quite often, as in *When I'm 64* (e.g., "Ev'ry summer we can rent a cottage in the Isle of Wight") and *Things We Said Today*. And Harrison's introspective, spiritual image is confirmed by his frequent use of words reflecting cognitive activity in songs such as *If I Needed Someone* (e.g., "you're the one that I'd be thinking of") and *Within You Without You* ("never glimpse the truth").

Linguistic Analysis of *Lucy in the Sky with Diamonds*

This research literature shows that that the linguistic style used in a particular piece of writing or speech is influenced by features of the author's personality (e.g., whether one is depressed and suicidal, whether one is Paul McCartney or John Lennon), by the author's current situation (e.g., whether one is lying, whether one is addressing an authority figure), and even by current societal events (e.g., whether one's country has just suffered a terrorist attack, whether it is the early or late 1960s). For this reason, merely running the LIWC program on *Lucy in the Sky with Diamonds* is unlikely to reveal anything very useful, as there would be no way to sort out how much the song's linguistic style was influenced by Lennon's personality, by his psychological situation at the time he was writing the song, or by the general era in which the song was recorded. For example, if the LIWC analysis revealed that *Lucy in the Sky with Diamonds* contained many negative emotion words, it might be that something about the themes on his mind at the time he was writing the song led Lennon to use such words frequently, or it might be reflective of his personality and typical songwriting style. Similarly, if *Lucy in the Sky with Diamonds* contains many big words, it might be that Lennon was intellectualizing at that particular time, or it might be that songwriters around 1967 used more big words in their songs, and Lennon was following that fad.

What is needed, therefore, is a group of songs whose linguistic styles can be compared to that of *Lucy in the Sky with Diamonds*. I therefore collected two such groups of comparison songs: the lyrics to other songs that Lennon had recorded in the previous year or so, and the lyrics to the no. 1 hit songs in the United States and the United Kingdom between January of 1966 and February of 1967. (See appendix A for a listing of all of these songs.) I then compared the LIWC scores for *Lucy in the Sky with Diamonds* to these two samples of songs. (Interested readers can find detailed results in appendices B and C.) If the linguistic style of *Lucy in the Sky with Diamonds* is basically similar to the linguistic styles of the songs in these two comparison groups, it would suggest that *Lucy in the Sky with Diamonds* was little different than other songs of the era and reflected nothing particularly special about Lennon's personality or about his psychological state at the time he was writing this particular song. If the linguistic style of *Lucy in the Sky with Diamonds* is different from the no. 1 hit songs but similar to other songs Lennon had recently been writing, it would suggest that the song's linguistic style mostly reflects Lennon's personality. Finally, if the linguistic style of *Lucy in the Sky with Diamonds* differs from the songs in both of these comparison groups, it would suggest that something about Lennon's psychological state at the time he was writing this particular song was primarily responsible for its linguistic style.

The results of the LIWC analysis show many ways in which the linguistic style of *Lucy in the Sky with Diamonds* is not especially different from the styles of the songs in the comparison groups. For example, the song is fairly typical in terms of its use of second and third person pronouns, and in its use of words concerning family, friends, achievement, money, religion, and the like. In these ways, the song appears to be typical of the songs Lennon and other musicians were writing during that era.

At the same time, there are numerous LIWC indicators on which *Lucy in the Sky with Diamonds* consistently differs both from songs Lennon had recently written and from other popular songs of the time. My understanding of the findings led me to classify these differences into three groups of indicators, as shown in Table 2.1.

The first group of indicators includes linguistic features that parallel what many people report experiencing when they take the drug LSD. For example, the cardinal feature of the drug experience is the presence of vivid visual hallucinations, in which colors and patterns seem to move through space and stable objects change their form unexpectedly. These types of experiences seem to be well-represented in *Lucy in the Sky with Diamonds*, as it scores consistently higher than many other popular songs of the era and songs Lennon had recently written in the percentage of words that concern *seeing* (e.g., "picture" and "eyes"), *motion* (e.g., "follow" and "drift"), and *space* ("in" and "down"). The song is also rather lower than these other songs in words that convey *certainty* (e.g., "always" and "never"). Certainty is often in doubt while people are under the influence of LSD, given how the drug changes their perceptual experiences.

Table 2.1. **Summary of Findings from the Linguistic Inquiry Word Count Analysis of** *Lucy in the Sky with Diamonds*

LIWC Indicator	Compared to Contemporary Lennon Songs	Compared to Contemporary No. 1 Songs in the UK and US
TYPICAL OF LSD TRIP		
Seeing	Somewhat High	Somewhat High
Motion	Somewhat High	Somewhat High
Space	Extremely High	Extremely High
Certainty	Somewhat Low	Low
Inclusive	Extremely High	Extremely High
Exclusive	Somewhat Low	Low
Ingestion	Somewhat High	High
IMMEDIACY VS. DISTANCING		
>6 Letters	High	Extremely High
First person singular pronouns	Somewhat Low	Very Low
Articles	High	Extremely High
Present tense verbs	Low	Very Low
Discrepancy	Somewhat Low	Somewhat Low
EMOTIONS		
Total Affect (Emotion)	Somewhat Low	Somewhat Low
Feeling	Somewhat Low	Somewhat Low

Note: The descriptions in this table are based on the z-scores presented in appendices B and C. Scores were considered *somewhat high* if the z-scores were between 0.80 and 1.20, *high* if the z-scores were between 1.20 and 1.60, *very high* if the z-scores were between 1.60 and 2.00, and *extremely high* if the z-scores were over 2.00. The same descriptors and cutoffs were used to characterize *low* scores if the z-scores were negative.

Users of LSD also often report what is known as an "oceanic feeling," a blissful experience in which the boundaries between themselves and others become less distinct, resulting in a feeling of connectedness with everyone and everything in the universe. These feelings of connection and the dissolution of boundaries are perhaps expressed in the song's lyrics through the high use of *inclusive* words (like "and" and "with") and the relative lack of *exclusive* words (like "but" and "without"). It is also tantalizing to note that, just as people typically take LSD by swallowing a small piece of paper infused with the chemical, words concerning *ingestion* (e.g., "eat" and "pies") occur more frequently in *Lucy in the Sky with Diamonds* than in the comparison songs.

While these findings are no doubt excellent fodder for those who claim that *Lucy in the Sky with Diamonds* is primarily about the experience of taking LSD, the song's linguistic style has other interesting linguistic features that suggest the song is not just "an acid song." In fact, five of the linguistic indicators on which *Lucy in the Sky with Diamonds* stands out map almost exactly onto one of the fundamental dimensions of language mentioned earlier in this chapter during the discussion of post-9/11 bloggers. This dimension of linguistic style, called *immediacy vs. distancing*, indexes the extent to which a person's language reflects being present in the here and now vs. separating oneself from what is happening at a particular moment. Research using the LIWC program has identified five specific linguistic features that cluster together to represent how immediate vs. distant a particular verbal expression is. More immediate language uses *first person singular* words (like "I" and "me") and *present tense* words (like "am" and "run"), whereas distanced language avoids such words, presumably in an attempt to direct one's awareness away from the experience of the moment.

The third linguistic indicator includes words that imply a *discrepancy* (like "would" or "should"). Immediate language uses such words, as they often relate some other state to the present (e.g., "I should have bought an apple instead of this candy bar"), whereas distanced language tends to avoid discrepancies. Immediate language also uses few *articles* (e.g., "a" and "the"), whereas distanced language uses many. This is probably because articles occur alongside concrete nouns (like "a river" or "the shore") that usually make reference to something outside of oneself. Finally, immediate language uses *shorter, simpler* words whereas distanced language uses longer, more complicated words (like "plasticine" and "tangerine"); this tendency likely reflects the fact that people often use abstractions and intellectualized language to avoid awareness of what they are actually experiencing in the moment.

What is remarkable about the LIWC results for *Lucy in the Sky with Diamonds* is that for each of these five indicators, the song consistently scores in the direction of being distanced rather than immediate. That is, compared both to other recent Lennon songs and to other recent popular songs, the lyrics of *Lucy in the Sky with Diamonds* have a relatively low percentage of first person singular pronouns, present tense verbs, and discrepant words, and a relatively high percentage of long words and of articles. Indeed, when I computed a summary score following the standard LIWC formula for combining these five indicators, the results showed that *Lucy in the Sky with Diamonds* is more distanced and less immediate than any of the songs Lennon had written in the previous year and than any of the no. 1 hits of the era.

The finding that *Lucy in the Sky with Diamonds* is a very distanced and non-immediate song is also consistent with the last set of indicators I will mention here: words expressing emotion and feeling. Recall that when Pennebaker used the LIWC program on the Beatles' songs, he found that Lennon used more words conveying unpleasant emotion than did McCartney or Harrison (2.43% of words vs. 1.49% and 1.96%, respectively). In regard to pleasant emotion, Lennon was more or less equivalent to his two bandmates (4.83% vs. 4.96% for both McCartney and Harrison), although he and McCartney both used fewer words expressing pleasant emotions in the songs they wrote on their own than in the songs on which they collaborated (7.90%).

Lucy in the Sky with Diamonds is almost stripped of emotion according to the LIWC results. Only 0.44% of the words in the lyrics convey positive emotion, and there are no words that the LIWC program recognizes as conveying negative emotion. The song also has no *feeling* words, i.e., words that reflect a bodily sense of connection to one's inner world (e.g., a gut feeling) or to the outer world (e.g., a caress or a punch). Both of these findings stand in contrast to the fact that while people are under the influence of LSD, they often report relatively strong emotions, both of the pleasant and not-so-pleasant varieties.

Summary

In some ways, the results of the LIWC analysis can be seen as consistent with the common claim that *Lucy in the Sky with Diamonds* is about the drug LSD, as several of the song's linguistic features parallel the visual hallucinations, constant flux, and awesome sense of connection that often characterize the experience of taking this drug. Other findings from the LIWC analyses, however, suggest that the drug explanation is limited. If the song were about an acid trip, one might expect that other linguistic features of the song's lyrics would be similar to what people report while taking the drug. Certainly Lennon had the ability at this point in his career to provide the listener with a reasonably accurate sense of what it is like to trip on acid, as he had done some months earlier in the song *Tomorrow Never Knows*.

But instead of reflecting the deep involvement in one's subjective experience and feelings that are typical of taking LSD, the lyrics of *Lucy in the Sky with Diamonds* are actually more similar to how people write and speak when they are lying and when they are attempting to psychologically distance themselves from painful psychological material. Rather than focusing on the experience of the here and now, the lyrics of the song avoid the self and the present, and instead focus on the abstract, the intellectual, and that which is outside of one's self. Moreover, rather than expressing the bevy of emotions that typically occur while one is tripping, and that Lennon often expressed in his other songs, *Lucy in the Sky with Diamonds* is almost barren of feeling. Emotions, of course, are notoriously "here and now," and rarely abstract.

In sum, these analyses of the linguistic style of *Lucy in the Sky with Diamonds* suggest that while Lennon was writing these lyrics, he may have been rather wary of engaging the present moment, his own inner experience, and his emotions.

3 | THE STORY

Humans have claimed any number of distinctions between our species and other animals: our upright posture, our opposable thumbs, our use of complex language, our use of tools, our invention of agriculture, and our self-awareness. Little by little, these supposed distinctions have been eroded by research showing that other primates stand upright and use their thumbs like we do; that gorillas, dogs, and some species of birds have reasonably large vocabularies and can comprehend the complexities of some grammatical rules; that chimpanzees, crows, and otters make and use tools; that ants farm and raise livestock; and that bottlenose dolphins, elephants, and the great apes recognize themselves in a mirror.

There is one distinction that has thus far stood the test of time, however: human beings are the animals who tell fictional stories. Our species seems to have begun creating and appreciating narratives thousands of years ago when our ancestors sat in caves or around campfires using protolanguages to share the details of their days. Eventually the tendency to create a narrative with a plot and characters led to stories about everything from the origin of the stars in the sky to how the little boy who wandered alone into the woods was eaten by the bogeyman. Stories like these bonded the group together, created culture, and taught the young. Today, stories remain a source of fascination for everyone from little children climbing into their parents' laps at bedtime with a book to the millions of adults who spend their time reading romance and mystery novels or watching weekly television sitcoms and dramas.

The tendency to take information and weave it into a narrative is also evident in many other, more hidden features of human life. Psychiatrist J. Allan Hobson, for example, claims that the form our dreams take emerges from the forebrain's attempt to create a coherent narrative out of random neuronal firings and eye movements. And other psychologists tell us that our "identities" are, at base, actually the stories each of us has created about our own lives: I saw her across a crowded floor on my first day of college, wooed and married her, and am now her husband; I passionately wanted to be a dancer, but when I lost my leg in a car accident I became a teacher instead; I was at the end of my rope until one day I stumbled into a church where a conversation with a minister led me to devote my life to Jesus.

If identities are indeed the complex stories people tell themselves about who they are, then the shorter stories people sometimes create might also reveal something fundamental about their identities. Indeed, this is the premise behind one of the most widely used psychological tests ever developed, the Thematic Apperception Test (TAT). The TAT is composed of numerous cards, all of which have simple pictures on them, such as a boy staring at a violin or an older man with a pipe leaning over a younger woman. After looking at a card, people are asked to tell a story that explains what previously happened, what is happening, and what will happen, as well as what each of the characters is thinking and feeling. Most individuals are able to quickly and easily come up with stories to these cards, and the resulting twists and turns in plot and character development have been shown to express important features of a person's identity. To take just one example, the TAT card with the picture of the boy and the violin is often coded for the presence of the *achievement motive*, or the desire to succeed. Individuals highly oriented towards achievement often make up a story in which the boy struggles but eventually masters this difficult instrument, whereas people less concerned with achievement typically develop a plot in which the boy ignores his parents' demands to practice and instead goes outside to play. Scores derived from this type of coding predict a variety of achievement-oriented behaviors in the laboratory and in "real life."

Another way to understand people through the stories they tell involves a process called "scripting," developed by psychologists Silvan Tomkins, Irving Alexander, and Amy Demorest. Scripting is an approach that attempts to lay bare the theme or pattern that underlies a particular story without relying on any particular theoretical lens for interpretation. The process the scripter goes through is relatively simple. First, the main character of the story is identified. Then the specific, literal words and images in the story are reduced down to the fundamental ideas that lie behind them. So, for example, if a boy told a story about coming into the living room and knocking over his brother's tower of blocks, the fundamental idea would be "I wrecked something." Finally, if the narrator happened to relate the events of the story in something other than chronological order, the scripting process requires arranging the fundamental ideas back into the order in which they would have occurred in real time.

While the scripts that result from this process might reflect concerns that are pressing on a person at a particular moment, they can also reveal fundamental themes and ideas that are basic to a person's "identity story." Consider, for example, how Amy Demorest and Paul Siegel used scripting to understand the identity of the famous American behavioral psychologist B. F. Skinner. Demorest and Siegel began their investigation with the first paragraph of Skinner's three-volume autobiography, *Particulars of My Life*:

> The Susquehanna River, named for an Iroquois tribe, rises in Otsego Lake in New York State. It flows southwest and south and crosses into Pennsylvania a few miles below the town of Windsor. Almost at once it meets a foothill of the Alleghenies, which proves unbreachable, and it abandons its southern course, swings west and north, and returns to the hospitable plains of New York State. It flows west past Binghamton and Owego and tackles Pennsylvania again at a more vulnerable point. This time it succeeds and, picking up the support of a large western branch, continues south past the state capital of Harrisburg and into Maryland and Chesapeake Bay, and so at last into the Atlantic Ocean.

Taking a narrative approach helps one recognize that Skinner started his autobiography with a little story about a river. Demorest and Siegel therefore considered the river to be the main character of this story, and then derived a script for this paragraph by abstracting the fundamental meaning behind the specific images and arranging them in sequential order. Here is the result:

I leave origins ⇒ meet barrier to progress ⇒ return to hospitable origins ⇒ I retackle barrier at a more vulnerable point ⇒ succeed in overcoming the barrier ⇒ pick up support ⇒ successfully achieve freedom

Next, Demorest and Siegel considered Skinner's description of the first psychological experiment he ever conducted:

It is not surprising that my first gadget was a silent release box, operated by compressed air and designed to eliminate disturbances when introducing a rat into an apparatus. I used this first in studying the way a rat adapted to a novel stimulus. I built a soundproof box containing a specially structured space. A rat was released, pneumatically, at the far end of a darkened tunnel from which it emerged in exploratory fashion into a well-lighted area. To accentuate its progress and to facilitate recording, the tunnel was placed at the top of a flight of steps, something like a functional Parthenon. The rat would peek out from the tunnel, perhaps glancing suspiciously at the one-way window through which I was watching it, then stretch itself cautiously down the steps. A soft click (carefully calibrated, of course) would cause it to pull back into the tunnel and remain there for some time. But repeated clicks had less and less of an effect. I recorded the rat's advances and retreats by moving a pen back and forth across a moving paper tape.

As the rat appeared to be the main character in this passage, Demorest and Siegel created the following script from the rat's point of view:

I am contained $\Rightarrow$ released from containment and encouraged to make progress $\Rightarrow$ cautiously emerge into freedom $\Rightarrow$ experience threats from authority $\Rightarrow$ I retreat to original containment $\Rightarrow$ repeated threats from authority $\Rightarrow$ decreased fear $\Rightarrow$ I advance

Comparing the two scripts shows that they share many similar underlying features: Something (the river, the rat) departs from a place of confinement (the Pennsylvania hills, the cage), encounters a barrier (mountains, experimenter), returns to its source (Pennsylvania, the cage), and ultimately obtains freedom. The repetition of this theme in both the first paragraph of Skinner's autobiography and in his description of his first experiment suggests that issues of personal freedom and confinement by others may have been particularly salient to his identity. And indeed, Demorest and Siegel found evidence for this fundamental script in several other areas of Skinner's life. For instance, it appears in his descriptions of childhood interactions with small animals and of a machine his parents made him use to improve his posture. The script comes up again in his autobiography when he describes the problems he encountered while living at home after graduating from college but before leaving for graduate school. And Demorest and Siegel also show how the script recurs during his middle life, when Skinner wrote his famous utopian novel *Walden Two* and seemed to project this fundamental theme onto the book's narrator, his namesake, Burris.

Script Analysis of *Lucy in the Sky with Diamonds*

If readers re-visit the lyrics of *Lucy in the Sky with Diamonds*, I think they will agree with me that the song clearly tells a story that includes characters and a plot. I therefore used the scripting method on the song's lyrics, starting with the assumption that the main character was "yourself." Here is the script I developed:

> I am traveling ⇒ I hear the voice of a remarkable female above me ⇒ but she leaves ⇒ I follow her ⇒ I enter a vehicle that brings me up ⇒ I find myself in a new traveling place ⇒ the remarkable female is nearby but still apart from me

When I constructed this script, I did my best to be objective and not to think about any theoretical ideas concerning Lennon or psychology. Nonetheless, the possibility remains that my own personality or my biases about Lennon could have influenced the resulting script. To address this possibility, Dr. Paul Siegel, co-author of the article on B. F. Skinner described above, graciously agreed to help me by writing his own script for the song. He did so with no knowledge of my script or of the themes I was exploring in this book. The script he wrote was:

> I am traveling ⇒ Divine beauty calls to me ⇒ I answer ⇒ I look for her, but she's no longer there ⇒ I am in awe ⇒ I follow her ⇒ I alter course and leave ⇒ But I am still in awe ⇒ I am traveling again ⇒ I see her again ⇒ I am in awe

While the two scripts are admittedly not word for word replicas of each other, they do share some common features. At base, both scripts suggest that *Lucy in the Sky with Diamonds* tells a story about someone who desires but does not quite attain union with a divine, awesome female figure. The main character is approached by this figure, but she disappears; the main character tries to follow her, and though she reappears, they remain separated.

The fact that Dr. Siegel and I derived similar scripts from the lyrics of *Lucy in the Sky with Diamonds* does not, however, indicate whether this theme of union and separation from a woman was of passing interest or enduring concern to Lennon. Perhaps events in his life around the time he was writing the song led Lennon to incorporate this script into *Lucy in the Sky with Diamonds*. For example, in late 1966 and early 1967, Lennon's first wife Cynthia was quite concerned that his LSD use was negatively influencing his mental health and their relationship; as such, the song might concern feelings of separation from her. On the other hand, perhaps the script reflected something more fundamental to Lennon's personality. If so, then similar scripts should be present in other songs Lennon had previously written.

A long tradition in psychology would suggest that examination of Lennon's very first songs should prove particularly fruitful in sorting through these possibilities. The idea that "what is first is foremost" can be traced back to the Viennese psychoanalyst Alfred Adler, who proposed that people's earliest memories reveal quite a bit about their psyches. Other psychodynamically influenced therapists put special stock in the first few sentences uttered by a patient or the first dream recalled during therapy, believing that such "firsts" often foretell the basic problems that will be encountered in treatment.

More recently, psychobiographer Irving Alexander identified a number of rules for deciding what material might be particularly useful when analyzing people's lives. "Primacy" was first among those rules, as Alexander noted that what is first is the "foundation stone" on which everything else in a life story is laid. Indeed, the reason that Demorest and Siegel scripted the first paragraph of Skinner's autobiography and his description of the first experiment he had conducted was that they were interested in whether or not the themes of Skinner's work connected with the themes of his life.

In the final major interview Lennon gave before his death, reporter David Sheff asked Lennon for his thoughts about almost every song in the Beatles' catalog. Lennon mentioned two songs as being among the first that he wrote: *Hello Little Girl* and *I Call Your Name*. (Before going further, readers may wish to peruse the lyrics of these two songs).

About *Hello Little Girl*, Lennon reflected:

That was actually my first song. {*Singing*} "When I see you every day I say mmm hmm, hello little girl." I remembered some Thirties or Forties song which was {*singing*} "You're delightful, you're delicious and da da da. Isn't it a pity that you are such a scatterbrain." {*Laughing*} That always fascinated me for some reason or another. It's also connected to my mother. It's all very Freudian. She used to sing that one. So I made *Hello Little Girl* out of it.

And about *I Call Your Name*, Lennon said:

That was my song. When there was no Beatles and no group. I just had it around. It was my effort as a kind of blues originally, and then I wrote the middle eight just to stick it in the album when it came out years later. The first part had been written before Hamburg even. It was one of my *first* attempts at a song (emphasis in original).

Following the same procedures as above, I created a script for the lyrics of *Hello Little Girl*:

I see a female ⇒ I want to be close to her ⇒ but she ignores me ⇒ I still hope for union ⇒ I reflect on other painful times ⇒ I still want union

I then created a script for *I Call Your Name* (omitting the bridge (or middle eight) that Lennon said he added years later):

I call out for you ⇒ but you are not present ⇒ I reproach myself and hide my pain ⇒ I call out for you

As before, these two scripts are by no means exact copies of each other or of the scripts Dr. Siegel and I each wrote for *Lucy in the Sky with Diamonds*. For instance, whereas the script for *Lucy in the Sky with Diamonds* contains no notable unpleasant feelings, the scripts for both of these early songs express distress about the singer's failure to be close to the desired person. Yet it is also clear that common to all of these scripts is a story about a person who wants to be united with someone who is not available: Lucy appears and is gone; the "little girl" entices but ignores the singer; and the object of the singer's desire in *I Call Your Name* has left and does not reply to the singer's pleas.

Summary

The scripting analysis undertaken here suggests that when he was writing *Lucy in the Sky with Diamonds*, Lennon was occupied with thoughts about connection to and separation from an incredible female figure. This theme does not seem to have been just a momentary concern of Lennon's, as the scripts derived from his two earliest songs tell a similar story about a person who wants to be near someone who remains far away. As such, *Lucy in the Sky with Diamonds* seems to have tapped into a concern about union and separation that had long been central to Lennon's identity.

4 | THE WORDS

Sigmund Freud related the following dream from one of his young female patients:

> She is sitting with her husband in the theatre; one side of the stalls is entirely empty. Her husband tells her that Elise L. and her fiance had also wanted to go, but had only got very bad seats, 3 for 1 flourin, 50 kreuzers, and of course they couldn't take those. In her opinion, that was no hard luck.

On the surface, this dream seems rather mundane—a woman and her husband go to a mostly empty theatre, and their acquaintances cannot get decent tickets. But Freud believed that deeper meanings lurk behind almost every dream, and that his method of *free association* could help extract these meanings, thereby providing insights about the dreamer's psyche. Freud's method is deceptively simple: the analyst identifies the primary images in the dream and the patient then shares whatever ideas, thoughts, feelings or memories that happen to come to mind regarding those images, no matter how tangential, ridiculous, or inappropriate the associations might seem.

When the young woman was asked to undergo this process, she reported the following associations:

(a) *The half-empty theatre*—One time she had been anxious to see a particular play, so anxious in fact that she had booked seats in advance and paid extra for that privilege. When she and her husband arrived to see the play, they found that she had "no need to be in such a hurry," as half of the auditorium was empty. Her husband often teased her about this occurrence.

(b) *Elise L.*—she had just learned that Elise L. had recently become engaged to be married.

(c) *3* (i.e., the number of tickets)—Elise L. was only 3 months her junior; she herself had been married for several years.

(d) *1 flourin, 50 kreuzers*—The day before the dream, her sister-in-law had been given 150 flourin (i.e., 100 times more money than the amount in the dream) by her own husband and had "been in a hurry" to spend the windfall on jewelry.

Freud's fundamental assumption was that the associations a patient gave to a dream provided clues as to the feelings, thoughts, and conflicts that might have precipitated the creation of the dream. He would therefore search for patterns in the dreamer's associations to see whether certain themes emerged. In this case, Freud noted two primary themes. First, his long-married but still young patient seemed to be implicitly comparing herself with a same-aged woman who was only now getting married. Second, themes of rushing into decisions too quickly seemed to come easily to mind for this patient. Freud therefore suggested to the young woman that perhaps she felt that she had been too hasty to rush into her own marriage—if only she had waited (like Elise L. did), perhaps she might have ended up with a better husband. Initially the woman rejected this interpretation of the dream, but as her analysis with Freud unfolded, she ultimately admitted that she did indeed harbor these kinds of thoughts and feelings.

Freud's theoretical ideas about how a dream is created have received relatively little empirical support, but contemporary research and theory in cognitive psychology support the potential usefulness of his method of free association. Hundreds of studies make it clear that any idea a person holds is part of a web of interconnected ideas, thoughts, and feelings, and that accessing any one idea affects the other ideas to which it is connected. One classic study demonstrated this interconnection by presenting people with strings of letters, some of which were words, like "d-o-c-t-o-r," and others that were nonwords, like "t-o-c-d-r-o." The study participants were told to press one key on a keyboard if the string formed a word and a different key if it did not, and to do so as quickly and accurately as possible. This task was actually a cover for the question the researchers truly wanted to investigate: Would people be quicker to recognize that a string of letters (such as "d-o-c-t-o-r") was a word if they had just seen a string of letters that formed a word closely associated with the target word (like "n-u-r-s-e") than a string of letters that formed a word that had little to do with the target word (like "p-i-z-z-a")? As expected, participants were indeed faster to recognize that "d-o-c-t-o-r" was a word if they had just seen "n-u-r-s-e," because in most people's web of associations, the concepts of "doctor" and "nurse" are much more closely connected than are "doctor" and "pizza." As such, when study participants saw "n-u-r-s-e," the part of their mind holding information about "medical personnel" and "hospitals" was activated, priming them to quickly recognize that "d-o-c-t-o-r" was a word.

Modern cognitive psychology might therefore suggest that Freud's patient created her dream in something like the following way. During the preceding day, she had been reminded of the idea of "rushing into decisions," perhaps by her sister-in-law's precipitous spending of the windfall gift. This sense of "rushing" also (unconsciously) reminded her of the earlier experience at the theatre with her husband, and contrasted with Elise L.'s decision to wait a bit longer to get married than she herself had. Because these images and concepts were interconnected in her mind, as her sleeping brain entered the dreaming state, her mind created a story out of these pre-activated images. Later, when she free-associated to the images of the dream, Freud was able to track the connections between the images and thereby identify the underlying theme embedded in the web of her associations.

Association Analysis of *Lucy in the Sky with Diamonds*

Freud's free association approach, supplemented by hundreds of research studies in cognitive psychology, suggests that whatever themes may have been present in Lennon's mind at the time he was writing *Lucy in the Sky with Diamonds* would have expressed themselves in the particular words, symbols, and images that Lennon ultimately used in the song's lyrics. If one were able to obtain Lennon's associations to each word in the song, these themes would likely be expressed across his associations, and thus become identifiable. Lennon is of course not available to lie down on a couch and provide these associations, so other methods of obtaining them are needed. Two hold some promise.

Personal Associations

One way to obtain a semblance of Lennon's potential associations to the words in *Lucy in the Sky with Diamonds* is to examine how he had used those words in earlier songs. A person's web of associations to a particular idea is based, at least in part, on past experiences that the person has had with that idea. For example, most people associate "doctor" closely with "nurse" because they have encountered the two ideas in close proximity multiple times. Similarly, the dream image of "a half-empty theatre" reminded Freud's patient of an actual event in her life, one associated with rushing unnecessarily.

Lennon would no doubt have had a variety of past experiences relevant to the many words and images that made their way into the lyrics of *Lucy in the Sky with Diamonds*. For instance, the fact that Lennon had been rereading *Alice in Wonderland* and *Through the Looking Glass* likely explains his appropriation of the words "boat," "marmalade," "rocking horse," "looking glass" and "train" from these books—those images had recently been primed in his mind. Other past experiences that Lennon would have had with the words in *Lucy in the Sky with Diamonds* include times when he had used them in the lyrics of other songs. Thus, it is reasonable to assume that the themes activated in Lennon's mind when he was writing the words to *Lucy in the Sky with Diamonds* share some commonalities with the themes that had been activated in his mind when he had used those same words in songs he had previously written.

I therefore set out to understand how Lennon had used the primary words that appear in *Lucy in the Sky with Diamonds* in earlier songs. My search found that he had used 22 of these words across 36 of his earlier songs. Some of these words had made their way into Lennon's lyrics only once before. Other words had shown up in about half a dozen songs. And one word, "girl," had appeared a dozen times.

Next, I sought to understand the context in which Lennon had used each word in the previous songs. I did so by reading the relevant line or set of lines in which the word appeared in an earlier song; I then summarized my best sense of the fundamental idea or feeling that was being expressed. Interested readers can check my judgments against their own by examining appendix D, which reports the places in the earlier songs where each of the 22 words from *Lucy in the Sky with Diamonds* had previously appeared, as well as the basic theme(s) that I identified as being associated with words in earlier contexts.

Through this process I identified eight themes that frequently reappeared in the context of Lennon's use of these words in earlier songs. Table 4.1 graphically represents the most prominent themes; the larger the theme's font size in the table, the more frequently words from *Lucy in the Sky with Diamonds* had appeared in the context of that theme in songs Lennon had previously written.

Three of the themes in Table 4.1 concern the intertwined ideas of separation, sadness, and death. Indeed, the single most frequently occurring theme identified was separation, reflected in words such as "call" ("I call your name, but you're not there"—*I Call Your Name*); "girl" ("I've got ev'ry reason on earth to be mad, 'cause I've just lost the only girl I had"—*I'll Cry Instead*); and "gone" ("If she's

Table 4.1. Themes potentially in Lennon's mind when he wrote *Lucy in the Sky with Diamonds*, based on an association analysis of his use of words in earlier songs

Separation	Away (×2) Call Down Girl (×4) Gone (×4) Head High (×2)	Look People (×2) Sky Someone Station Take Tree
Love	Diamonds Eyes (×2) Girl (×5) High	Look People Somebody (×3) Someone
Sadness	Down (×6) Eyes Gone (×2)	Head (×2) Sky Take (×2)
Comfort	Away Call (×3) Down (×2) Look	Somebody (×3) Someone Sun
Hiding	Appear Away (×2) Eyes Girl	Green Head (×2) People
Insulting Relationship	Down (×2) Flowers	Girl Look
Jealousy	Down Girl Green	Head Look
Death	Call Girl Head (×3)	

gone I can't go on"—*You've Got to Hide Your Love Away*), among many others. Feelings of sadness, a common emotional response to loss, are also prominent in the lyrics of many earlier songs that contain words Lennon used in *Lucy in the Sky with Diamonds*; these include words such as "down" ("feeling low down"—*Good Morning, Good Morning*); "eyes" ("Ev'ry night the tears come down from my eyes"—*It Won't be Long*); and "sky" ("My tears are falling like rain from the sky"—*I'm a Loser*). And death, one of the ultimate separations, had apparently been on Lennon's mind when he used several of the words that later appeared in *Lucy in the Sky with Diamonds*, including "call" ("Nothing to do to save his life, call his wife in"—*Good Morning, Good Morning*) and "girl" ("Well I'd rather see you dead little girl, than to be with another man"—*Run for Your Life*).

Another cluster of themes revolves around ambivalent feelings toward interpersonal relationships. Lennon had previously used many of the words in *Lucy in the Sky with Diamonds* in the context of having or desiring a loving relationship. For example, a sense of love and connection is conveyed in his earlier use of the words "girl" ("I'm so glad that she's my little girl"—*I Feel Fine*); "someone" ("If you want someone to make you feel so fine, then we'll have some fun when you're mine all mine"—*Little Child*); and "people" ("Tho' I know I'll never lose affection for people and things that went before"—*In My Life*), among many others. Further, words from the lyrics were also frequently associated with the theme of comforting or being comforted, as is the case for "away" ("If the sun has faded away, I'll try to make it shine"—*Anytime at All*) and "somebody" ("Leave it all 'til somebody else lends you a hand"—*Nowhere Man*).

But this association analysis also suggests that thoughts of jealousy had been prominent in Lennon's mind when he previously used some of the words that appear in *Lucy in the Sky with Diamonds*, as with "down" ("If I catch you talkin' to that boy again, I'm gonna let you down and leave you flat"—*You Can't Do That*) and "girl" ("Well I'd rather see you dead little girl than to be with another man"—*Run for Your Life*). And Lennon had also used both "down" and "girl" (among other words) when describing an insulting woman (e.g., "She's the kind of girl who puts you down when friends are there"—*Girl*).

A final theme identified through this process echoes one of the findings from the LIWC analyses reported in chapter 2. Recall that the linguistic style of *Lucy in the Sky with Diamonds* was typical of "distancing" language that avoids the present moment and emotions. In a similar way, this association analysis revealed that several words Lennon used in the lyrics to *Lucy in the Sky with Diamonds* had previously been used in the context of hiding one's feelings and one's self. Some examples include the words "appear" ("I'm not what I appear to be"—*I'm a Loser*); "away" ("Hey, you've got to hide your love away!"—*You've Got to Hide Your Love Away*); and "head" ("If the rain comes they run and hide their heads"—*Rain*).

Common Associations

As creative an individual as John Lennon was, he still had much in common with the average human being. He breathed and slept, loved and sometimes felt afraid. And he almost certainly would have been more likely to associate the word "doctor" with the word "nurse" than with "pizza." The web of associations that made up his particular mind would no doubt have had its idiosyncrasies, but it also would have shared much with other speakers of the English language.

As such, a second way to understand the potential associations that may have been activated in Lennon's mind when he was writing *Lucy in the Sky with Diamonds* is to understand what most people would associate with the words that he used in the song's lyrics. Happily, an excellent data set on common free associations is publicly available, provided by cognitive psychologists at the University of South Florida who have spent years asking people to share the first word that comes to mind in response to hundreds of different words, including 20 of the 22 words used in the personal association analysis conducted on *Lucy in the Sky with Diamonds*. This comparison sample is admittedly not a perfect fit for our purposes, given that the associations were provided by U.S. college students sitting in a laboratory in the 1980s and 1990s rather than by young British musicians writing songs in the 1960s. However, the data should at least provide some sense of the associations to these words that may have been present in Lennon's mind. The most common associations these college students gave are listed in appendix E, and the common themes that emerged across those associations are summarized in Table 4.2.

Many of the same themes identified in the personal association analysis also appear in the common associations that the college students had to these words from *Lucy in the Sky with Diamonds*. For instance, the intertwined themes of separation, sadness, and death emerge in associations to words like "away," "gone," and "down." And the theme of hiding is relevant to two associations for the word "appear."

Table 4.2. Themes present in the free associations of college students
to those words from *Lucy in the Sky with Diamonds* that Lennon had
also used in previous songs

Theme	Lennon's Word: Common Associations
Separation	**Appear:** Disappear, vanish **Away:** Gone, go, leave, goodbye **Gone:** Left, away, went, disappear, leave, bye, goodbye, lost **Take:** Away, leave
Love	**Diamonds:** Engagement **Flowers:** Love **Girl:** Friend **People:** Friend, nice, like
Drugs	**Head:** Pot, shop **High:** Drug
Death	**Gone:** Dead **Sky:** Heaven
Hiding	**Appear:** Seem, hide
Sadness	**Down:** Depressed, out

The common associations also reflect the positive aspects of
loving relationships that were found in the personal association
analysis. This similarity is evident in the associations to "diamonds,"
"flowers," "girl," and "people." Missing from these common associations, however, are the more negative feelings of jealousy and being
insulted that also emerged in Lennon's personal association analysis. Perhaps this feeling of ambivalence about relationships is less

characteristic of the average college student's associations to these words than of Lennon's associations. This suggests such associations were either basic to Lennon's personality or to his experience at the time he was writing these songs.

Finally, it is worth mentioning that college students commonly provided associations to two of the words—"head" and "high"—that were relevant to drugs. Such a finding resonates well with the common interpretation that *Lucy in the Sky with Diamonds* is about the hallucinogen LSD.

Summary

The analyses used in this chapter combined Freud's method of free association with contemporary research in cognitive psychology in an attempt to understand the themes and concerns that may have been on Lennon's mind when he was writing *Lucy in the Sky with Diamonds*. The idiosyncratic ways in which Lennon had previously used the same words in other songs and the common associations college students have to those words both suggest that more distressing themes may have lain underneath the seemingly pleasant lyrics of *Lucy in the Sky with Diamonds*. Themes of separation, sadness, and death were identified in the students' associations and in Lennon's previous use of many of the words. A sense of hiding one's self and one's true feelings was also apparent in both sets of associations.

These analyses also converged on the possibility that positive ideas and feelings about interpersonal relationships were active in Lennon's mind when he was writing *Lucy in the Sky with*

Diamonds, as such associations emerged in Lennon's previous songs and in the common associations of college students. However, the students did not seem to express the more negative, ambivalent feelings about relationships that were identified through examination of Lennon's earlier songs. This could mean that these particular aspects of the associations identified in Table 4.1 are not so common but were instead more idiosyncratic to Lennon's own web of ideas.

Lastly, the fact that associations to drugs were identified in the common associations to two of the words in *Lucy in the Sky with Diamonds* but not in Lennon's own associations is consistent with the fact that many people believe the song is about drugs while Lennon himself repeatedly denied that interpretation.

In sum, the analysis of the personal and common associations to words from *Lucy in the Sky with Diamonds* suggests that when Lennon was writing these lyrics he may have been concerned with separation, sadness, and death, with hiding his feelings, and with both positive and negative aspects of intimate relationships.

5 | THE MUSIC

*L*ucy in the Sky with Diamonds is, of course, a song, so a full analysis of the meaning it might have had for Lennon cannot rely solely on examining its words—attention to the music is also required. This chapter uses a strategy like the one developed in the previous chapter, but applied to the music of *Lucy in the Sky with Diamonds*. Specifically, I identified some fundamental musical characteristics of *Lucy in the Sky with Diamonds* and then searched Lennon's earlier songs for similar features, following a process akin to how I identified the words in *Lucy in the Sky with Diamonds* and then sought to find how Lennon used those words in previous songs. Songs that share many musical features with *Lucy in the Sky with Diamonds* might be particularly revealing of what was on Lennon's mind while he was composing the music to this song.

Although it may seem odd to take a method based on associations to words and apply it to music, psychological research suggests the feasibility of such an approach, as auditory information appears to be stored in memory in ways not fundamentally dissimilar to how verbal information is stored. This is why when one hears a siren or a particular person's voice, one can bring to mind relatively quickly what that sound means, as well as ideas about the source of the sound. Furthermore, studies document that listening to music can activate specific memories of one's life, particularly memories that are emotional and social.

Recent studies have even examined the brain structures involved in recalling memories activated by music. College students in one such study listened to short clips of easily recognizable songs from their adolescence (e.g., *Hollerback Girl* by Gwen Stefani and *I Gotta Feeling* by the Black Eyed Peas) and then retrieved an autobiographical memory relevant to each song. This entire procedure occurred while their brains were being scanned by a Magnetic Resonance Imaging machine. Attesting to the power of music to bring memories to mind, the analyses revealed that the portions of the brain suggested by previous research to be "turned on" during the process of remembering events from one's life (e.g., portions of the temporal lobes and the hippocampus) were indeed activated after listening to clips of popular music.

Perhaps more importantly for understanding the potential associations of a singer-songwriter like Lennon, the actual physical movements involved in creating certain sounds seem to be deeply and unconsciously embedded in people's nervous systems. These "procedural memories" hold information that allow people who practice actions like typing a common word, dancing a complicated step, or riding a bicycle to eventually undertake those actions without consciously thinking about them. Similar processes also seem to be at work for musical actions like picking out notes on a piano or strumming a sequence of chords on a guitar. Indeed, case studies of amateur musicians who developed Alzheimer's disease reveal that such individuals can continue to play songs on their instruments even when they can no longer remember the names of those songs and when they have difficulty performing simple tasks like dressing themselves or waving goodbye when asked to do so. Such findings argue strongly that memories for how to perform songs occupy specific locations in the brain.

This research in cognitive neuroscience suggests that when Lennon played or sang a particular sound or sequence of sounds while he was writing the music to *Lucy in the Sky with Diamonds*, memories of similar sounds or sequences of sounds present in his earlier songs may have been activated in his mind, as would the actual physical actions necessary to have created those sounds.

Musical Analysis of *Lucy in the Sky with Diamonds*

Finding musical features in Lennon's earlier songs that are similar to those of *Lucy in the Sky with Diamonds* presents certain challenges, because every song has multiple musical features that could be analyzed in multiple ways. In an attempt to keep this analysis reasonably straightforward, I chose to examine four basic musical features of *Lucy in the Sky with Diamonds*: (1) the time signature of the song, (2) the key in which it was performed, (3) its melodic themes, and (4) its chord progressions. (Again, readers may want to listen to *Lucy in the Sky with Diamonds*, or perhaps obtain a musical transcript of it, before going deeper into this chapter).

One basic piece of information a performer needs to know about a piece of music is the song's time signature, or how many beats occur in each measure of the song. Most popular Western songs of the 1960s, and most songs Lennon had previously written, are in "standard" or 4/4 time, meaning that there are four beats per measure (as in, for example, *Anytime at All* or *I Saw Her Standing There*). *Lucy in the Sky with Diamonds* has two unusual features with regard to its time. First, it begins in 3/4 time, meaning that there are 3 beats per measure (like most waltzes). The second unusual feature in terms of time is that the song changes time signature from 3/4 to 4/4 (at the 75th measure, right before the refrain begins). Thus, I counted a song Lennon had previously written as being musically similar to *Lucy in the Sky with Diamonds* if it began in 3/4 time or if the time signature changed during the song.

Another piece of information a performer needs to play a song is the key in which it is written. Every key has its own distinct sound and feel because of the particular notes and chords (i.e., combinations of notes) that are frequently used in that key—this is partly why a song like *Blackbird* sounds so different from *Come Together*. The performer of written music knows which key to use by looking for the presence or absence of sharps and flats at the start of the song's transcription; an accomplished performer who can play by ear often can pick up the key of the song just by listening to the song's dominant tones. *Lucy in the Sky with Diamonds* begins in the key of A-major (which has three sharps). Thus, being written in the key of A-major is one fundamental feature of the song, because if the song was in a different key (e.g., C-minor), it would have both sounded different and required that Lennon engage in a different set of movements to produce those sounds. Most pop songs remain in the same key for their duration, but that is not true for *Lucy in the Sky with Diamonds*: it switches key twice, first (at the 24th measure) to the key of B-flat major (which has two flats) and then again (at the 75th measure) to the key of G-major (which has one sharp). Thus, for the analysis regarding key, I considered a song that Lennon had previously written as being similar to *Lucy in the Sky with Diamonds* if it was written in any one of these three keys or if the key changed at some point during the song.

A third typical feature of any song is its melody, the succession of notes that determines "the tune," or how most people recognize that one person is humming *Love Me Do* but another is humming *Happiness is a Warm Gun*. Three melodic themes stand out as particularly characteristic of *Lucy in the Sky with Diamonds*. The first theme is the repeating sets of three stepwise descending notes (the same motif as the melody of *Three Blind Mice*) which appear over and over throughout the first portion of the song (e.g., in measures 6–9, measure 11, and measures 15–19). The second theme occurs later in the song when a single note is repeated over and over, first 6 times in a row (measures 24–25), then 7 times in a row (measures 28–30), and then 10 times in a row (measures 32–35); this sort of repetition of a single note was rather typical of Lennon's style, showing up in songs like *Girl* (e.g., when he sang "She's the kind of girl who puts you down when friends are there"). The third musical theme that characterizes the melody of *Lucy in the Sky with Diamonds* is a long, 7-note stepwise descent that occurs during the refrain "sky with diamonds" (e.g., measures 37–38); this is similar to Lennon's enunciation of the first "I" and the word "do" in "Whenever I want you around yeah, all I gotta do" from *All I've Got to Do*. I therefore looked for any of these three melodic patterns in Lennon's previous songs.

The final feature of *Lucy in the Sky with Diamonds* that I examined concerns the song's chord progression and bass line. In most popular songs the notes (alone or in combination as chords) that are played "below" the melody occur in a sequenced way (i.e., the progression or line) that depends upon the key and the time signature so as to support the melody sung "above." Many popular Western songs of the 1960s were based on repetitions of a few chords with their corresponding bass notes—for example, the structure of *Twist & Shout* includes notes derived from the progression of three chords (i.e., I, IV, and V) that are repeated in the same order over and over and over throughout the song. *Lucy in the Sky with Diamonds* is once again not so simple, as the chord progression (or the corresponding bass line) changes along with the key in each portion of the song. Because there is no clear sequence established in the portion of the song written in B-flat-major (e.g., measures 24–35), it would be difficult to confidently say that a similar pattern was notable in another song. The progression during the refrain in G-major (e.g., measures 37–42) is likewise not very useful for the current purposes, as this section of *Lucy in the Sky with Diamonds* utilizes a progression so common in blues and rock-and-roll songs (i.e., a pattern based on the standard I-IV-V sequence) as to render it lacking much distinction. The only progression of chords and corresponding bass notes in *Lucy in the Sky with Diamonds* that seems both stable and unique enough to make it worth looking for in other songs occurs during the part of the song written in A-major (e.g., measures 5–17). Here, the song's bass line is organized around a sequence of chromatically descending chords, starting with A, then dropping to G, F-sharp, F-natural, and E, before repeating the descent again from G. I therefore counted another song Lennon had written as being similar to *Lucy in the Sky with Diamonds* if it included a chord progression with a similar stepwise descent.

All told, I searched Lennon's previous songs for eight musical features that appeared in *Lucy in the Sky with Diamonds*: (1) beginning in the 3/4 time signature; (2) a change in time signature; (3) use of the key of A-major, B-flat-major, or G-major; (4) a change in key; (5) a melodic sequence involving a stepwise three-note descent; (6) a melodic sequence involving frequent repetition of a single note; (7) a melodic sequence involving a long stepwise descent of notes; and (8) a chord progression involving a stepwise descent. Each song Lennon had written before *Lucy in the Sky with Diamonds* was scored for the presence of each of these eight musical features.

Many of Lennon's earlier songs share one, two, or even three of these eight musical features with *Lucy in the Sky with Diamonds*, but two songs stand out as particularly similar, as each shares four musical features with *Lucy in the Sky with Diamonds*. These two songs are *Help!* and *Strawberry Fields Forever*. Interestingly, Lennon once identified these two as "the only true songs I ever wrote." Appendix F presents the musical commonalities between each of these songs and *Lucy in the Sky with Diamonds*.

Having identified the two songs that seem most similar musically to *Lucy in the Sky with Diamonds*, the next step was to understand what they might have meant to Lennon so as to identify the psychological ideas and feelings that may have been on his mind when he was writing the music to *Lucy in the Sky with Diamonds*.

Help!

Lennon wrote *Help!* approximately two years before *Lucy in the Sky with Diamonds* when he was asked to compose a song with this title for the Beatles' second feature-length movie. As Lennon recalled in his final major interview before his death, the song came out of him "bam! bam!, like that…" Two dominant themes are present in the song's lyrics, both of which are expressed alongside some of the musical features of *Help!* that overlap with *Lucy in the Sky with Diamonds*.

A sense of depression is the first theme clearly present in *Help!* For example, Lennon sings about his lack of confidence and his insecurity during the repetitive, single note melodic theme that is characteristic of both *Help!* and *Lucy in the Sky with Diamonds*. Later, he vocalizes the word "down" in the same descending, stepwise, three-note melodic sequence that was repeated so frequently in *Lucy in the Sky with Diamonds*. Lennon's reflections fifteen years after he wrote *Help!* also explicitly mention how depressed he had been at the time:

> It was my fat Elvis period. You see the movie: He—I—is very fat, very insecure, and he's completely lost himself (sic). And I am singing about when I was so much younger and all the rest, looking back at how easy it was…I was fat and depressed and I *was* crying out for help (emphasis in original).

The strong need for a relationship is the second theme in the song's lyrics that coincides with the musical elements shared between *Help!* and *Lucy in the Sky with Diamonds*. For instance, Lennon's pleas for *Help!* occur both during the frequent repetition of a single note and during the stepwise descending chord progression (e.g., "Help! I need somebody, Help! Not just anybody..."). And near the end of the song, Lennon sings "Please, please help me" in two sets of the descending, stepwise, three-note melodic sequence that would later be prominent in the melody of *Lucy in the Sky with Diamonds*. As with the theme of depression, feelings of being disconnected and desiring help from someone also emerge in Lennon's later reflections on *Help!* He recalled that:

> We were smoking marijuana for breakfast during that period. Nobody could communicate with us because it was all glazed eyes and giggling all the time. In our own world. The whole Beatle thing was just beyond comprehension.... When *Help!* came out, I was actually crying out for help.

Strawberry Fields Forever

Lennon began writing *Strawberry Fields Forever* a few months before *Lucy in the Sky with Diamonds*, over a period of several weeks in the fall of 1966 while he was in Spain acting in the movie *How I Won the War*. The song was released on the flip side of McCartney's *Penny Lane* as a dual musical memory of their childhoods; in fact, the original sleeve for that 45 record featured pictures of the Beatles as children.

The lyrics to *Strawberry Fields Forever* are quite a bit more obscure than those of *Help!*, and many music critics have commented on the sense of dislocation and confusion that the words and the music both convey. Musically, the points in *Strawberry Fields Forever* that are most similar to *Lucy in the Sky with Diamonds* occur in the first two measures of each of the verses (e.g., "Living is easy with eyes closed," "No one I think is in my tree"). In these measures, the same note is repeated over and over in the melody and a backing chord progression is used that follows a descending stepwise sequence similar to that of *Lucy in the Sky with Diamonds*.

Themes concerning separation seem to dominate the lyrics in these portions of *Strawberry Fields Forever*. For example, "Living is easy with eyes closed" seems to reflect the benefits of shutting out the world and of denying a connection with that which is around you. And the line "No one I think is in my tree" again expresses a sense of being alone and away from others. Lennon's own comments on the song, shared more than a dozen years after writing it, reiterate these themes. In his final major interview, Lennon said that the line "Living is easy with eyes closed," was an attempt to express how, throughout his whole life, he had felt more "hip" and "different" than others. This theme continued into Lennon's reflections about "No one I think is in my tree…":

> What I'm saying, in my insecure way, is "Nobody seems to understand where I'm coming from. I seem to see things in a different way from most people."

When asked by the interviewer whether he ever "found people who shared your visions," Lennon replied, "Only dead people in books. Lewis Carroll, certain paintings I would see."

It must also be noted that the inspiration for the title of *Strawberry Fields Forever* comes from a Salvation Army orphanage near the home of Lennon's Aunt Mimi. An orphanage, by definition, is a place for children who are separated from or who have lost their parents. As we shall see in the next chapter, this orphanage must have held a special fascination for the young Lennon, as he had moved out of his parents' home and in with his Aunt Mimi after his father "ran away to sea" and his mother "couldn't cope with me."

Summary

Chapter 4 began with the assumption that when Lennon was choosing the words for the lyrics of *Lucy in the Sky with Diamonds*, certain ideas and feelings had been activated in his mind that were associated with those words. As such, some information about those ideas and feelings could be obtained by understanding how Lennon had used those same words in previous songs. The analysis used in the current chapter made a similar assumption, namely that the features that Lennon used in the music of *Lucy in the Sky with Diamonds* were connected in his mind with past songs he had composed in which he had heard similar sounds and had made similar movements to create those sounds. On this basis, I sought to find the songs most similar musically to *Lucy in the Sky with Diamonds*, as they seemed especially likely to reveal something useful about his psychological state at the time he wrote this particular song.

Help! and *Strawberry Fields Forever* were identified as the two songs that shared the most musical features with *Lucy in the Sky with Diamonds*. Interestingly, the themes expressed in the lyrics of these two songs revolved around some of the same concerns and ideas that emerged from earlier analyses, namely concerns about feeling depressed, having a desire for connection, and being separated from others. It is also particularly interesting to note that these themes were often expressed lyrically during the very portions of *Help!* and *Strawberry Fields Forever* that were especially similar musically to *Lucy in the Sky with Diamonds*. Specifically, Lennon sang about feeling sad, separated, and desirous of connection at some of the very points in these two songs that shared melodic themes and chord progressions with those that he would use again months later when he was writing *Lucy in the Sky with Diamonds*.

6 | THE MAN, HIS RECENT PAST, AND HIS SON'S PICTURE

Imagine that a ball rolls down a sidewalk and hits a stick lying in its path. As a result of this event, the ball's trajectory is diverted in a particular way. If you wanted to understand the trajectory the ball took after it hit the stick, you would need at least three types of information.

First, you would need to know something about the ball, such as its density, mass, and size. Was it a bowling ball? A Ping-Pong ball? A beach ball?

Second, you would need to know something about the recent temporal context of the ball's travels so that you could understand its state when it hit the stick. Had the ball been accelerating, decelerating, or rolling at a constant speed? Was the sidewalk smooth or bumpy? At what angle was the ball traveling relative to the stick?

Third, you would need to know something about the stick, as contact with the stick was the event that led the ball to change its trajectory. Is the stick larger or smaller than the ball? Is it shaped in a way that the ball could go over or under it, or that it would send the ball in a particular direction?

Once you compile and integrate all of this information, you would be better positioned to understand why the eventual trajectory of a Ping-Pong ball traveling uphill and hitting a large branch head-on would differ from the trajectory of a bowling ball rolling downhill and hitting a twig at an angle.

Understanding the trajectories that lives take is obviously far more complicated. Humans have many more working parts than do balls, the context of their recent experiences is often quite complex, and they can make any number of meanings out of the events they encounter. Nonetheless, understanding why a particular individual does a particular thing at a particular time is facilitated by the same kinds of information needed to understand the trajectory a ball takes after rolling into a stick.

Having shed some light in chapters 2 through 5 on the trajectory Lennon took in writing *Lucy in the Sky with Diamonds*, the next task is to describe the particulars that brought this song into being. Figure 6.1 presents a schematic representation of these factors. First, John Lennon's personal history must be understood, as the personality structures formed earlier in his life would have influenced how he wrote the song. Second, the recent temporal context of Lennon's life must be described, as events that occurred in the months before he wrote *Lucy in the Sky with Diamonds* would have affected his state of mind at the time of the song's composition. Third, the meanings that Lennon may have made from the specific event that precipitated the song's composition must be uncovered, as something about his four-year-old son's picture set in motion the chain of events that resulted in this song. To be clear, it was the confluence and interaction of these three sets of factors that ultimately determined why Lennon wrote *Lucy in the Sky with Diamonds* and why this song has the characteristics identified by the analyses presented in chapters 2 through 5.

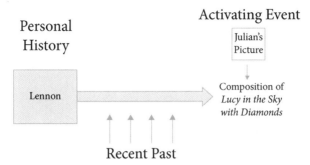

Figure 6.1 Types of information needed to understand Lennon's composition of *Lucy in the Sky with Diamonds*.

Lennon's Personal History

John Lennon was born in Liverpool to Julia (nee Stanley) and Freddie Lennon on October 9, 1940, amidst the onset of World War II. His parents had wed, against the bride's family's wishes, almost two years earlier. Lennon was conceived not long before his father went to sea on a series of merchant marine voyages dodging German U-boats to bring supplies into Britain. Although by most accounts Julia was a warm, vivacious, playful woman who enjoyed being with her young son, with her husband away she began carousing around the pubs of Liverpool; one biographer claims she sometimes left the young Lennon alone at night in a dark apartment for hours on end while she was out flirting and drinking.

Eventually Julia struck up a relationship with a British soldier and became pregnant by him in the fall of 1944. When Freddie returned from one of his many voyages and found out what had happened, he took the young Lennon from Julia, sending the boy to live with his own older brother, Sydney. The young Lennon stayed with his Uncle Sydney and Aunt Madge for several months, and the couple began to hope that they could eventually adopt him. But after Julia gave birth to her child in June of 1945, Freddie retrieved his son and the two moved in once again with Julia. This reunion did not last long, however, as Julia developed a relationship with yet another man, John Dykins, for whom she left Freddie. The young Lennon was apparently quite upset at this turn of events and took a dislike to the new man in his life, perhaps because he occasionally saw Dykins behaving violently toward his mother. Around this time, Lennon also began running away, sometimes to the nearby home of his mother's sister, Mimi.

One time when Lennon showed up at his aunt's door in the spring of 1946, Mimi called Lennon's father and asked him to come retrieve his son. Freddie was about to ship out on a voyage, but a couple of weeks later, he gathered Lennon and brought him to Blackpool, a beach resort town in the northwest of England. There the father and son spent several weeks together, during which time Freddie devised a plan to emigrate with his young son to New Zealand. But Julia tracked him down that June and demanded that her son return home with her to Liverpool. After witnessing an argument between his parents, the five-year-old Lennon was told to choose the parent with whom he wanted to stay. Initially he turned to his father, but as the boy watched Julia leave, he ran to follow his mother. It would be two decades before he saw his father again.

His reunion with Julia did not last long, as within weeks the young Lennon had moved into the quiet middle-class home of his childless Aunt Mimi. Explanations of this event vary. Some stories suggest that Julia willingly handed her son over to Mimi; others portray the change as being brought on by child-welfare officials disturbed by the boy's home situation; and still others claim that Mimi essentially stole Lennon after Julia came to her home bloodied from a beating by Dykins. Whatever combination of events actually occurred, Lennon spent the bulk of his childhood and adolescence living with his stern and structured Aunt Mimi and his passive but affable Uncle George.

Aunt Mimi did her best to instill middle-class behaviors and ideals into her young charge, insisting on regular meals and baths, as well as proper manners. She also exposed him to classical music, religion, and a library of British literature, including the Lewis Carroll books that later helped inspire *Lucy in the Sky with Diamonds* and other songs. While he did take in some of what Mimi tried to teach him, Lennon's mischievous and sometimes aggressive streak still emerged in school and in his romps around the neighborhood with friends. He picked up the habits of trespassing and shoplifting, as well as an acerbic, sometimes vicious, tongue. He was in almost constant trouble at school for various offenses, often for cutting classes. And as he entered his teen years, he discovered both sex and popular music.

Lennon's burgeoning love for Elvis Presley, Little Richard, and other singers of the early rock-and-roll era was scorned by Aunt Mimi but supported by his mother. While he had seen relatively little of Julia in the years after he moved in with Mimi and George, the teenaged Lennon began spending more and more of his free time at his mother's nearby home. By most reports, the music was always on at Julia's; she purchased and played new popular records from the United States, and she even bought the jeans and shirts Lennon hankered for to make his "Teddy boy" image complete. After he formed his first band, the Quarrymen, Lennon and his bandmates often practiced in her home, and Julia was in the audience at their first concert in the fall of 1956.

While he continued his musical development with the Quarrymen and brought Paul McCartney and George Harrison into the band, Lennon also entered art college. Despite some natural drawing talent, Lennon's rebellion had increased to the extent that many of his instructors considered him unteachable. It was here that he would meet both Stu Sutcliffe, the man who would become his best friend in his late adolescence, and Cynthia Powell, who would become his first wife. It was also during this period that, in Lennon's words, "the worst thing that ever happened to me" occurred.

On Sunday July 15, 1958, his mother Julia was killed in a car accident. She had been to Mimi's for tea, an almost daily tradition for the reconciling sisters. Lennon had been out all afternoon and was, ironically, at Julia's home awaiting her return. Julia and Mimi said their goodbyes, and a friend of Lennon's who had stopped by, Nigel Walley, walked with Julia to the nearby bus stop. After they parted, Julia pushed through the hedge into Menlove Avenue and was struck by an oncoming automobile. Mimi heard the sound of the collision all the way back at her home and rushed to join Walley at the scene of the accident. They found Julia with massive head wounds, but still breathing. She was quickly taken to the hospital but died soon after.

In the interviews he conducted with Hunter Davies between 1966 and 1967, Lennon recalled:

> I was staying with Julia and Twitchy (Lennon's nickname for Julia's common-law husband, John Dykins) this weekend. We were sitting waiting for her to come home, Twitchy and me, wondering why she was so late. The copper came to the door, to tell us about the accident. It was just like it's supposed to be, the way it is in the films. Asking if I was her son, and all that. Then he told us, and we both went white. It was the worst thing that ever happened to me. We'd caught up so much, me and Julia, in just a few years. We could communicate. We got on. She was great. I thought, fuck it, fuck it, fuck it. That's really fucked everything. I've got no responsibilities to anyone now. Twitchy took it worse than me. Then he said, "Who's going to look after the kids?" And I hated him. Bloody selfishness. We got a taxi over to Sefton General where she was lying dead. I didn't want to see her. I talked hysterically to the taxi-driver all the way, just ranted on and on, the way you do, just babbled on. The taxi-driver just grunted now and again. I refused to go in and see her. But Twitchy did. He broke down.

The car that killed Julia was driven by Eric Clague, a 24-year-old off-duty policeman who only had a learner's permit. Witnesses differed in their reports as to whether Clague was speeding and driving recklessly before he hit Julia; ultimately the official report of Julia's death implied that she herself was at fault for not looking before walking into the roadway. Julia's family never accepted this explanation, feeling that the officials at the inquest took the side of Clague.

Lennon initially responded that night to the news of Julia's death by crying in the arms of a girlfriend and then playing his guitar on the front porch. By the time of Julia's funeral a few days later, however, he lay numb with his head in the lap of his cousin Liela, neither speaking nor moving. Opportunities for further grieving seem to have been blocked by the avoidant and stoic responses of his family members. Julia's two young daughters were at first told that their mother was alive but in the hospital, and then were sent to relatives in the north of Britain. It was not until several weeks later that they were finally told their mother had died. Lennon's aunts, including Mimi, expressed little in the way of open grief, and, according to Lennon's soon-to-be girlfriend and first wife Cynthia, "Julia had become a taboo subject and no one mentioned her. The family dealt with pain by keeping it under wraps."

Although he may have talked a bit with his bandmate Paul McCartney, whose own mother had died from cancer a year previously, Lennon acted the tough, non-emotional teenage boy with most of his peers. Lennon's good friend Pete Shotton said "he never showed it…He never gave anything away." One incident in particular is telling. A month or two after Julia's death, a fellow art student yelled, "Hey, John, I hear your mother got killed by a car." Lennon is said to have replied, "Yeah, that's right." According to the individual who witnessed this event, "he didn't register anything. It was like someone had said 'You had your hair cut yesterday.'" Instead of expressing his emotions or talking about his pain, by all accounts Lennon's primary means of coping with his mother's death became hiding the sadness and anger he felt, drinking copiously, and being verbally and physically aggressive to those around him.

Analysis of Lennon's Personal History: Attachment Theory

Many different theoretical approaches could be used to understand how Lennon's personality developed out of these (and other) experiences from his childhood and adolescence. One approach that seems to stand out as particularly relevant and useful in the case of Lennon is called *attachment theory*. Developed in the 1960s, attachment theory was created by John Bowlby in an attempt to integrate (1) the psychoanalytic approach in which he had been trained, (2) research literature on the relationships of young animals with their caregivers that had emerged in the 1950s, and (3) his own experiences working with British children who had been separated from their parents during World War II. The ideas that Bowlby came to propose in his classic three-volume work on attachment and loss (titled respectively, *Attachment*; *Separation*; *Loss*) have been remarkably influential across several subdisciplines of psychology, generating thousands of research studies, and yielding one of the best-validated sets of ideas for understanding how children's development and personality are affected by their early experiences with caregivers.

Bowlby began by drawing on the work of animal researchers such as Konrad Lorenz (with geese) and Harry Harlow (with monkeys), which suggested that many young animals come into the world with a predisposition to attach themselves to a caregiver.

In humans, this basic motive emerges quite strongly around the time children start crawling and is evidenced by their tendencies to protest when separated from their caregivers and to cling to them upon reunion. These and other behaviors serve at least two crucial functions: to keep increasingly mobile children near the caregiver at a time when they could endanger themselves by wandering off, and to help children receive the comfort and "emotional refueling" they need throughout the day (and night).

Cross-cultural studies show that most caregivers meet their children's attachment needs by sensitively responding to their children in warm and consistent ways, thereby helping the children to develop what Bowlby called a "secure" attachment style. In their interactions with caregivers, children with secure attachment styles come to learn that they are loveable and that other people are trustworthy; as such, these children develop a strong sense of self-esteem that allows them to confidently function in the world. They also typically believe that others will be available to provide them with comfort when it is needed.

Not all children are so fortunate. Research shows that children with caregivers who are rather cold and undemonstrative develop what is called an *avoidant* attachment style, as they learn that their attempts to seek solace are likely to be rebuffed or met with half-hearted compliance by the caregiver. For these reasons, avoidant children are often hyper-independent, eventually developing the attitude that "I can take care of myself and don't need anyone else."

Still other children are raised by caregivers who are highly inconsistent, sometimes showering the infant with love, but other times being physically or emotionally unavailable to help soothe

the child. Research suggests that such parenting often leads these children to develop an *anxious/ambivalent* attachment style (or what is also called a *resistant* or *preoccupied* attachment style). These children learn from their interactions with their caregivers that while other people can occasionally help or soothe them when they are feeling bad, they should not be too confident that those people will consistently be available. These disruptions in the attachment relationship also leave such children relatively unable to soothe themselves when they are upset, for they have not had the kinds of caregiving experiences that facilitate the development of this capacity. As a result, anxious-ambivalent children are understood to have a *hyper-activated* attachment system, because they have stronger-than-normal desires for relationships that might give them the soothing they cannot give themselves. These children often come to feel rejected because of their parents' inconsistencies, thereby raising questions in their minds about how loveable they are. Negative beliefs about themselves, in turn, can cause them even more distress, thus locking these children into a distressing cycle, as they have difficulty both soothing themselves and finding people who are consistently available to help soothe them.

Much about Lennon's experiences in the first five years of his life would have predisposed him towards developing an anxious-ambivalent style of attachment. From the point of view of a young boy trying to understand his world, the experiences he had with caregivers must have seemed rather bewildering. His father was repeatedly present and then absent throughout the first couple of years of Lennon's life. His mother seemed to like to play with him, but, if the reports of biographers can be trusted, all too often he awoke alone in a dark room and called for her in vain. He was taken from his mother's home to live with an aunt and uncle, and then, after a few months, yanked back to his mother's home, where he soon found her living with a new and sometimes violent man. Soon after that, he was again separated from his mother when his father took him to the beach resort. Then, after being forced to make a choice between his parents (a choice that no five-year old has the cognitive or emotional capacity to make), he paid the price of a seemingly permanent separation from his father, who left his life entirely for years. And on the heels of this abandonment, the mother he *had* chosen to stay with gave him up yet again, this time for years. Essentially, the near-constant refrain of Lennon's first five years was union followed by separation, a style of care that is proto-typical of the disruptions in parenting consistency that are known to create anxious-ambivalent attachment styles in children.

Beliefs about others and themselves that children derive from their earliest experiences do not disappear as they age, according to attachment theory, but become part and parcel of their developing personalities, even into adulthood. Thus, it is possible to provide further evidence that Lennon may have developed an anxious-ambivalent style of attachment by considering the extent to which he exhibited the various features that research has shown characterize such individuals. Generally speaking, the match is strong.

For example, children with this attachment style are likely to be angrier and behave more aggressively than children with the other two primary attachment styles. Lennon clearly acted out physically and verbally throughout his childhood and adolescence. Research has also shown that the problems with self-esteem and relationships that are basic to an anxious-ambivalent attachment style lead people with this style to suffer more from depression and anxiety. Whether one reads descriptions of Lennon's personality provided by his three main lovers (Cynthia, Yoko, and May Pang), his friends, his biographers, or Lennon himself, everyone seems to agree that Lennon was a rather insecure, anxious, and vulnerable man. Given the difficulty they have soothing their negative emotional states either on their own or through relationships, people with anxious-ambivalent attachment styles use more alcohol and other drugs as a way to "self-medicate" and blunt their emotions. Indeed, Lennon was a frequent user of one drug or another from adolescence on, once saying, "I've always needed a drug to survive." Researchers have also examined the kinds of adult love relationships associated with different attachment styles; once again Lennon fits the characteristics of an anxious-ambivalent pattern. Such individuals are known to be especially jealous that their lovers might cheat on them, a problem his first wife Cynthia encountered throughout their relationship, even as Lennon was frequently cheating on her. People with this attachment style also tend to be quite clingy in their relationships, desiring almost constant connection with their romantic partners; nothing could better describe the inseparability that Lennon eventually exhibited with Yoko Ono, as the two were almost joined at the hip for years after the initiation of their affair.

Analysis of Lennon's Personal History: Grief

An analysis of Lennon's reaction to his mother's unexpected death is also crucial to understanding his personality. As described above, Lennon's immediate response seems to have reflected both the anger and sadness most people would naturally feel upon hearing the news that a loved one had been killed. After that first night, however, Lennon seems to have shut off his expression and experience of pain. In large part, this was probably due to the interpersonal and cultural environments in which Lennon found himself, environments that clearly discouraged him from continuing to express how he felt. Not only was he surrounded by the famous stoicism of British culture, but the people in his immediate social environment largely held back their tears and actively stifled further discussion about Julia, going so far as to hide her death from her daughters for weeks. Lennon had little choice but to follow the pattern set by his family.

Most theorists, going back at least to Freud, agree that experiencing and expressing one's painful and unpleasant feelings are necessary to "successfully grieve" and come to a satisfactory sense of closure with regard to one's relationship with the deceased. Indeed, some researchers suggest that the opportunity to talk through one's feelings about the deceased is particularly important when a death is sudden and unpredicted; such events can be quite difficult to make sense of on one's own. What's more, males in particular benefit from having the chance to talk about their emotions after a death, because otherwise they tend to focus on "getting back to normal." Between the choice of his family to close off all discussion about Julia and his "tough-guy" image in a culture that encouraged stereotypical masculine behavior, Lennon was not likely to continue crying about his mother's death for long. Instead, it was much more acceptable for him to avoid his feelings by getting drunk and into fights.

These dynamics were likely complicated further by Lennon's early experiences with his mother. Recall that an initial impetus for Bowlby's studies of attachment was to understand how people, especially children, react to separation and loss. Researchers have examined these connections, conducting dozens of studies on how grief and attachment styles relate. Psychologists R. Chris Fraley and Phillip R. Shaver summarized this literature:

> [There] is considerable empirical support for Bowlby's idea that chronic mourning stems from an anxious-ambivalent attachment organization. He believed that lack of responsiveness on the part of attachment figures (in both childhood and adulthood) heightens an individual's vigilance and sensitivity to cues regarding separation, rejection, and loss. As a result, when irretrievable losses occur, anxious-ambivalent or preoccupied individuals have difficulty resolving these losses because their attachment systems are primed to continue yearning and searching for the missing attachment figures.

The problems associated with "irretrievable losses" for anxious-ambivalent individuals are even more acute when they attempt to suppress their thoughts about separation, as Lennon seems to have done. In one research project, for example, study participants were asked to imagine that an important relationship had ended, and some of the participants were encouraged to try to suppress their resulting thoughts and feelings. All study participants then wrote in a stream-of-consciousness style, and the researchers looked for themes of loss in the prose that subjects had generated. Suppression seemed to work for individuals with an avoidant attachment style, as their prose revealed fewer themes of loss. However, suppression clearly backfired for those with an anxious-ambivalent style, as themes of loss actually *increased*.

Lennon was obviously a complex man, and there was certainly much more to his personality than I have attempted to present here. But it also seems clear from these analyses that Lennon was a person with long-standing beliefs that interpersonal relationships typically end in separation, a deep yearning for connection to others, and a fragile sense of self. Further, it seems likely that he carried within him a lingering, unresolved set of painful emotions about his mother's death, feelings that he typically attempted to avoid experiencing.

The Recent Past

After his mother's death, Lennon went on to became a full-fledged musician, form the Beatles, marry, father a child, release albums, make films, and become world-famous. While all of these intervening events are no doubt important in their own right, here I will focus on the events of 1966 so as to understand how the recent temporal context may have affected Lennon's psychological state as he entered the winter of 1966–1967, encountered Julian's picture, and composed *Lucy in the Sky with Diamonds*. Those months were clearly a time of flux for Lennon, marked by internal and external turbulence of many sorts.

As noted earlier, Lennon had long been a regular and heavy user of a host of drugs: cigarettes, alcohol, marijuana, uppers, and downers. In January of 1966, Lennon began seriously experimenting with the hallucinogenic drug LSD. Although he had taken

LSD a couple of times before (first unknowingly ingesting it in a spiked cup of coffee), Lennon now started tripping regularly, sometimes multiple times per week. On occasion he did so while reading Timothy Leary's *The Psychedelic Experience*, a guidebook based on the *Tibetan Book of the Dead* and designed to promote the user's psychological and spiritual development; Lennon liberally borrowed from this book to write the lyrics of *Tomorrow Never Knows*. These frequent forays into a chemically altered state of awareness left his wife Cynthia feeling more and more isolated from Lennon, as well as worried about his mental health.

Then in July, some fans who had once so adored Lennon and the Beatles turned against him with fury. The first instance occurred in the Philippines, when Brian Epstein (the Beatles' manager) ignored an invitation for the Fab Four to visit the presidential palace. The perceived snub of their leaders led hundreds of angry Filipinos to form a gauntlet at the airport through which the Beatles had to run to their plane; punches, kicks, and even bricks were thrown at the Beatles and their entourage. Later that summer there was trouble of a different sort in the United States, when an interview was published in *Datebook* in which Lennon proclaimed that the Beatles were "more popular than Jesus now" and that "I don't know which will go first—rock-and-roll or Christianity." While readers in the United Kingdom had more or less ignored Lennon's comments when they had been published a few months earlier in the *Evening Standard*, youth and adults in the southern United States were infuriated. Throughout the Bible Belt, Beatles' albums and memorabilia were piled into pyres and set aflame, and Lennon received at least one death threat. Then the reaction spread across the world, as the playing of Beatles' music was banned in South

Africa, Holland, and Spain, and the Pope criticized Lennon in the Vatican's newspaper. At first confused by these reactions, Lennon soon became quite upset, as he and his bandmates worried about the feasibility of completing their upcoming world tour in such an atmosphere. Eventually Lennon apologized and tried to explain what he had intended by his comments.

Around this time Lennon also received a warning from a psychic that while he was in the United States, he would be shot. This premonition fanned Lennon's fears about his safety, especially since the Beatles were scheduled to play multiple shows in the country. Nonetheless, he toured North America through threatening remarks of the Ku Klux Klan, a bomb scare, and firecrackers thrown on stage while he was playing.

The Beatles finished the tour in San Francisco that August. It would be their final live concert, marking the end of a half dozen years of nearly constant performing and touring. Lennon had never particularly enjoyed touring, so at one level he was happy to see a halt to the grind. At the same time, by most accounts he was rather lost as to how to fill the hole this would create in his life.

He responded that fall by cutting his famous mop-top hair, donning what would become his trademark "granny glasses," and heading to Spain to play the role of Private Gripweed in the film *How I Won the War* (where he began the composition of *Strawberry Fields Forever*). Later that fall he returned home to London and his LSD trips.

Analysis of the Recent Past

Clearly, the months leading up to the day when Lennon first saw Julian's picture were far from tranquil. Indeed, from a psychological perspective, the types of events that had recently occurred in

Lennon's life could not have been better designed to destabilize and stress a person. Lennon had quickly gone from three years of stupendous success and glorification by the world to people throwing bricks at him, setting fire to his albums and pictures, and threatening his life. The sense of confusion brought on by these stresses surely must have been amplified by the cessation of touring. Similar to the way that many men have difficulty adjusting when they retire, the end of touring seems to have led Lennon to feel unsure about who he was and what he would do with his life. Indeed, Lennon later recalled thinking, "I couldn't deal with not being onstage. [For] the first time I thought, 'My God, what do you do if this isn't continually going on. What else is there?'"

Importantly, these stresses and life transitions occurred in the context of Lennon's frequent ingestion of one of the most powerful mind-altering drugs known to science. In comparison to the tens of thousands of studies conducted on other psychoactive drugs, relatively little is understood about the effects of LSD and the other major hallucinogens, in large part because around 1970 many nations decided to classify them as "Schedule I," thus greatly limiting researchers' access to these drugs. Nonetheless, studies from the 1950s and 1960s, as well as a handful of more recent studies, suggest that Lennon's existing personality structures were likely to have been significantly perturbed by his many trips on LSD.

Lennon himself commented on this, claiming the LSD had "destroyed my ego." This statement seems in many ways an apt description. From what the research shows about LSD, its physiological, neurochemical, and psychological effects parallel the experience of psychosis, when people lose touch with reality and their sense of self and are often overwhelmed by irrational thoughts, feelings, and concerns. Lennon certainly reported some psychotic-like symptoms, noting that he "was very paranoid in those days, I could hardly move" and that "I didn't believe I could do anything…I was just nothing, I was shit."

At the same time, Lennon also seems to have experienced some of the known benefits of the drug. For example, studies with volunteers show that ingestion of LSD increases the likelihood of experiencing "oceanic boundlessness," a blissful state in which a person feels at one with the universe; even months later, many study participants consider this aspect of their laboratory trip to be among the most personally and spiritually significant experiences in their lives. Such experiences were among the reasons that Lennon gave for using LSD.

The possibility that LSD can change people's conceptions about who they are is supported by studies that have administered the drug in combination with close guidance and support from a sober individual. This type of "psychedelic" or "psycholytic" therapy has been demonstrated to be useful in helping terminally-ill cancer patients come to grips with their imminent deaths, as well as in treating anxiety disorders. The effectiveness of this type of treatment is understood by some practitioners to hinge upon LSD's ability to dismantle patients' psychic defenses, thereby allowing them to more quickly access, experience, and work through unpleasant emotions and conflicts that derive from occurrences in early life and from current existential concerns. Some recent neurological research supports this proposal, suggesting that the combination of psychotherapy with closely monitored administration of hallucinogens results in changes in brain structures (or what is called "neuroplasticity") in the prefrontal lobe. This area of the brain seems to be the best candidate for the organic seat of identity and the ego, according to neuroimaging studies.

Although Lennon was not taking LSD while under the supervision of a professional therapist, it seems reasonable to conclude that his use of LSD may have had parallel effects on him—a general weakening of his established identity and defensive structures, paired with increasing access to psychological material that he may have pushed outside his awareness. The likelihood that such processes were occurring for Lennon would have been enhanced by the recent stresses in his life (e.g., the death threats) and the major transition brought on by the end of an activity around which he had organized much of his time (i.e., touring).

The Activating Event

There was an actual moment in Lennon's life when his son Julian handed him a picture of a girl named Lucy who was up in a diamond-filled sky. This picture of Julian's (which can be seen on the cover of his EP *Lucy*) is rendered primarily in tans, with splashes of crimson and a bit of pale green. Lucy herself appears on the left third of the page beside some crimson zigzags. The girl's body is clearly outlined and seems to float, as no ground is visible. Above Lucy's body is an obscure green spot that may be her face, as slightly above it on either side are two prominent, eye-like objects drawn in red. Immediately next to Lucy, in approximately the middle of the page, Julian drew a circle with tipped points coming off its edge. This sun-like motif is also repeated at the top right of the page, this time surrounded with diamond-like shapes.

While no obvious boat-like form appears in Julian's picture, something about the picture made Lennon think of the Lewis Carroll books he so loved, as he claimed that the song's "imagery was Alice in the boat." Lennon appears to have been referring to Carroll's poem, *A Boat beneath a Sunny Sky*, which ends the book *Through the Looking Glass*. Lennon clearly adopted the river setting of this poem (reproduced in Box 6.1) as the starting point for his lyrics. He also incorporated words such as "sky," "sun," and "eye" that both appear in the poem and are easily recognizable in Julian's picture.

Another noteworthy feature of the event that set in motion the composition of *Lucy in the Sky with Diamonds* is that the artist was Julian, Lennon's own son. Julian's mother, Cynthia (Powell), had been dating Lennon for years when she discovered in the fall of 1962 that she was pregnant. In her memoir, Cynthia relates what happened when she first told Lennon that she was pregnant:

> He went pale and I saw the fear in his eyes. For a couple of minutes we were both silent. I watched him as I waited for a response. Would he walk out on me? Then he spoke: "There's only one thing for it, Cyn. We'll have to get married." I asked him whether he meant it. I told him he didn't have to marry me, that I was prepared to manage on my own, but he was insistent. "Neither of us planned to have a baby, Cyn, but I love you and I'm not going to leave you now."

Soon after, Lennon and Cynthia married in what the bride described as a "carbon-copy of John's parents' wedding twenty-four years earlier." For months, the marriage was kept secret from the popular press, as the Beatles' manager, Brian Epstein, was concerned that the band would lose some of its female following if news leaked out that one of the boys had a wife.

Box 6.1

Lewis Carroll's *A Boat beneath a Sunny Sky*

A Boat, beneath a sunny sky
Lingering onward dreamily
In an evening of July—

Children three that nestle near,
Eager eye and willing ear,
Pleased a simple tale to hear—

Long has paled that sunny sky:
Echoes fade and memories die:
Autumn frosts have slain July.

Still she haunts me, phantomwise,
Alice moving under skies
Never seen by waking eyes.

Children yet, the tale to hear,
Eager eye and willing ear,
Lovingly shall nestle near.

In a Wonderland they lie,
Dreaming as the days go by,
Dreaming as the summers die:

Ever drifting down the stream—
Lingering in the golden gleam—
Life, what is it but a dream?

Lennon was on tour when Cynthia went into labor in April of 1963, and it was not until Julian was three days old that father and son met for the first time. The newborn boy was named John Charles Julian Lennon, an amalgamation honoring his father John, his mother's father Charles, and his father's mother Julia. After a quick visit to the hospital, Lennon promptly left again to resume touring with the Beatles. Not long after, he returned to his family for a week or so, and then, when Julian was three weeks old, Lennon departed for a vacation to Spain with Epstein. Thus the pattern of Lennon's relationship with his son Julian was quickly established: brief interactions punctuated by extended absences while Lennon was on tour, in the studio, or on the set of a movie. Even when he was at home, Lennon's interactions with Julian were quite limited—Cynthia described her husband as being "present but absent."

The fact that Julian was not a planned child seems to have forever colored Lennon's perception of this relationship. After Cynthia and Lennon separated in the late 1960s, Julian went months at a time without hearing from his father. Even near the end of Lennon's life, when he was contrasting the birth of his and Yoko's son Sean with that of Julian, Lennon said:

I'm not going to lie to Julian. Ninety percent of the people on this planet, especially in the West, were born out of a bottle of whiskey on a Saturday night, and there was no intent to have children. So ninety percent of us—that includes everybody— were accidents. I don't know anybody who was a planned child. All of us were Saturday-night specials. Julian is in the majority, along with me and everybody else...I don't love

Julian any less as a child. He's still my son, whether he came from a bottle of whiskey or because they didn't have pills in those days. He's here, he belongs to me, and he always will.

Analysis of the Activating Event

Two features of this event stand out, both of which concern childhood.

First, childhood nursery rhymes play important roles in Julian's picture, Carroll's poem, and Lennon's song. Julian's picture was created while he was at nursery school, and the title is essentially a transposition of the line "Like a diamond in the sky" from *Twinkle Twinkle Little Star*. Lennon also reported that Julian's picture and title reminded him of a poem by Lewis Carroll, whose writings began engrossing Lennon soon after he moved in with his Aunt Mimi while a young boy. The last stanza of Carroll's poem refers to lines from another well-known nursery rhyme, *Row Row Row Your Boat*, as the characters drift "down the stream" and the author ends with the question "Life, what is it but a dream?" And the tune of the nursery rhyme *Three Blind Mice* formed the basis of parts of the melody of *Lucy in the Sky with Diamonds*.

Second, this picture of a girl in the sky had not been sent to Lennon in the mail by some unknown Beatles fan, nor had Lennon happened to spot the drawing in an art gallery. The picture was created by an almost four-year-old boy named John Charles Julian Lennon. While it is admittedly speculative to suggest that thoughts and feelings about his own boyhood might have been activated in Lennon's mind during this interaction with Julian, there are numerous pieces of evidence that suggest this may have been the case. First, his son shared both Lennon's own name and that of Lennon's dead mother. Second, Lennon clearly identified both himself and his son as accidentally conceived, "born out of a bottle of whiskey on a Saturday night." Third, Lennon's relationship with Julian had, at that point, more or less recapitulated Lennon's relationship with his own parents: Just as Freddie had been away at sea for much of Lennon's early years, Lennon was away for most of Julian's childhood, pursuing the life of a famous and busy musician. And just as Lennon had been the recipient of sporadic attention from both of his parents, Lennon was now similarly inconsistent in his relationship with Julian, sometimes showering him with toys and affection, but more often ignoring or being separated from his son. Fourth, it is tantalizing to note that at the time Julian presented his father with the drawing of Lucy, the boy was approximately the same age that Lennon had been during his first prolonged separation from his mother (i.e., when Julia was pregnant by the British soldier and Lennon's father took the boy away to live with Lennon's Uncle Sydney) and was only a year or so younger than Lennon had been when both his father, Freddie, and his mother, Julia, disappeared for years from his life.

Summary

Although more of the biographical events of Lennon's life could be discussed, I believe enough information has now been provided to sketch out a plausible explanation of how Lennon came to compose *Lucy in the Sky with Diamonds* in the manner that he did at the time that he did. That is the purpose of the next chapter.

7 | RECIPE FOR A SONG

Begin with a man who has been carrying within him since his earliest years a particular set of beliefs about relationships. His experience with his parents throughout his childhood and adolescence taught this man that one cannot confidently rely on relationships, as, for him, painful separation almost inevitably follows from union. At the same time that he holds these beliefs, this man has a more desperate yearning for connection with other people than does the average person, needing relationships to help soothe him during the many times when he feels bad. And when his relationships fail to work well in this regard, he often turns to drugs as a means of numbing himself and escaping from his reality.

Add to the mix of these concerns a deep and abiding sense of loss from his mother's accidental death when he was a teenager, an event that reinforced his beliefs about relationships, given that it occurred not long after he had regained contact with her following years of separation. Ensure that between the norms of his culture, the stoicism and strange responses of his extended family to his mother's death, and his own "tough guy" image, the man copes with his grief by continually pushing aside the sadness and anger he feels. Given his particular psychic structure, these attempts at suppression ironically keep those feelings quite alive in his mind.

Take this man with this personality, let him age some, and then give him dozens upon dozens of doses of a powerful hallucinogenic drug whose documented effects include psychotic-like symptoms, destabilization of identity and defense mechanisms, and increased access to long-standing but often suppressed emotional conflicts. Just to make sure that the man is sufficiently stirred up, at the same time as he is regularly taking this drug, stress him further by subjecting him to massive public criticism, by threatening his life, and by having him stop one of the primary activities that had for years organized his work life. Together, the drugs and stresses will increase the strength and accessibility of the man's beliefs about relationships and his feelings about his mother's death at the very time that he has fewer psychological resources than usual to cope with these conflicts.

In the midst of this confusing and difficult time, present the man with a picture drawn by a young boy. Have the young boy be the man's son, and have the boy's name be a melding of the man's own name and that of his dead mother's. Have the young boy be of approximately the same age that the man had been when he himself experienced the first prolonged separation from his own mother. Top this off by having the picture the boy draws be of a girl in the sky, so as to remind the man of a powerful female who is "above him," difficult to reach, or possibly even in heaven. Doing so will increase the likelihood that when this boy gives the man this picture, the concerns about relationships and about his mother's death that have become increasingly accessible in the man's mind will become even more insistent.

Add color to the man's reactions to this picture by bringing to his mind a poem he had read as a child and that he had been recently re-reading. Allow the images of "boat," "eye," "sky," and "sun" from that poem to percolate in his consciousness and seem worthy of incorporation into the song he has begun to write in response to the boy's picture. Ensure that even as the man consciously uses these images from the poem, deeper in his mind he also remembers the poem's more mournful lines: "Echoes fade and memories die," "Still she haunts me, phantomwise," "Never seen by waking eyes," and "Dreaming as the summers die." Even deeper still, connect somewhere in his mind the lines "In an evening of July" and "Autumn frosts have slain July" with the facts that July not only shares a linguistic root with the names of his son and his dead mother, but was the month in which his mother had been killed almost nine years earlier.

If these conditions are met, when the man decides what the song is to be about, he will create a story depicting a person who seeks to be close to this woman in the sky but who never quite attains union with her. This plot is the basic script that has been fundamental to the man's understanding of relationships since early childhood, figuring in the very earliest songs that he wrote. The script appears in this song now because it has been activated once again by the stressful, mind-shaking experiences of the prior months combined with this picture of a female in the sky drawn by a boy who reminds the man of his mother and of himself as a boy.

As the man chooses the words to the lyrics, the style of language he uses will reflect many of the perceptual characteristics of the experience of taking hallucinogens, given how much time he has recently spent in states that distort his senses. More importantly though, the man will use language in the song that avoids emotional content and is of the sort that people often use when they are trying to protect and distance themselves from the here and now. Although the man has written about his emotions in past songs without using such distanced language, at this particular point in time he is struggling with memories and feelings about his mother and her death, and his long-entrenched strategy for avoiding these concerns emerges. As such, he includes words in the song's lyrics that he previously used when he had explicitly described hiding from his feelings and being fake, and he writes the lyrics in a style that helps him evade the strong feelings about his mother that he has not yet been able to resolve.

Despite these efforts, the difficulties of the past few months and the lure of the boy's drawing will have given such strength to the underlying memories and feelings about his mother and her death that the man also finds himself drawn to words he had previously used in songs concerning the loss of relationships and a desire for union. Some of the words he uses in the lyrics will reflect the ambivalence he feels about women, given the way his mother sometimes loved him but at other times ignored and abandoned him. Other words will reflect the loneliness and depression with which he has long struggled. And still other words will be connected in his mind with the idea of death.

And as the man sets his lyrics to music, his mind will gravitate toward the same kind of sounds, musical structures, and musical phrases that he had heard, sung, and played on his piano and guitar when he had previously written about the kind of themes that were occupying his mind while writing this song. As such, he chooses a key signature, background chord progressions, and melodic themes similar to those he used in earlier songs whose lyrics concerned depression, feelings of isolation, and the desire for connection to someone.

In this way, it seems, John Lennon came to write *Lucy in the Sky with Diamonds* in the winter of 1966–1967.

8 | THE NEXT SONGS

At the point in their psychotherapy when clients begin to open the door on psychologically painful topics, they often vacillate between wanting to open that door further and wanting to close it tight once again. On the one hand, certain psychological processes seem to impel people toward further expression and exploration of whatever pain they have begun to describe. These processes, however, are countered in many cases by tendencies to push aside those thoughts, feelings, and memories so as to avoid the distress that contemplation of them engenders and the difficult changes in one's life that full exploration would typically entail.

The analysis presented in chapter 7 suggests that the circumstances of Lennon's life around the time he was writing *Lucy in the Sky with Diamonds* were such that he began to express his long-suppressed feelings about his mother and her death, albeit in an emotionally blunted way that was veiled behind hallucinogenic imagery. Said differently, the form the song took seems to have been a compromise between Lennon's desire to express and his desire to defend against that expression. This explanation of Lennon's creation of *Lucy in the Sky with Diamonds* can be tested by looking at what happened in the months that followed. Specifically, to the extent that circumstances in Lennon's life were of the sort that would maintain (or increase) the accessibility of these painful feelings and that would weaken his typical means of coping with these feelings, Lennon would be expected to continue to write songs that refer to his mother and to the constellation of ideas and feelings that surrounded her in his mind. Given that when he was writing *Lucy in the Sky with Diamonds*, Lennon appeared to have been quite wary of deeply exploring and explicitly expressing these concerns, this tendency toward expression should be quite tentative, at best. On the other hand, to the extent that the circumstances of Lennon's life changed so as to encourage a return to his typical approach of suppressing his expression of these concerns, a drop in references to his mother should be notable.

The Last Half of 1967

In the months soon after the Beatles completed their recording of the songs for the *Sgt. Pepper's Lonely Hearts Club Band* album, circumstances in Lennon's life seem to have continued to support further exploration of his feelings about his mother and her death. Two sets of events from the summer of 1967 are particularly noteworthy.

First, Lennon continued his frequent ingestion of LSD; some have suggested that he was almost constantly tripping during this period of his life. As described in chapter 6, research suggests that Lennon's heavy use of this drug would likely have weakened his defenses further and increased the accessibility of the deep, emotional, psychological material that seems to have begun to be expressed in *Lucy in the Sky with Diamonds*.

Second, the Beatles' manager Brian Epstein died in August of 1967, probably from a drug overdose. While Epstein had been less and less involved in the Beatles' daily lives since the band had stopped touring the year before, and while Lennon's cruel barbs were often aimed at Epstein's ethnic heritage (Jewish) and sexual orientation (homosexual), it is also clear that of all the Beatles, Lennon was closest to Epstein. Lennon is reported to have reacted to the news of Epstein's death as he had to the deaths of his Uncle George (in 1955) and of his best friend Stuart Sutcliffe (in 1962)—hysterical laughter followed by emotional numbness. And although Lennon and the other Beatles clearly seemed shaken by their manager's death and did visit Epstein's mother to express their condolences, they did not attend Epstein's funeral and instead quickly went into business meetings to discuss their next steps forward as a band.

Late that summer, with LSD coursing through his brain and death primed in his mind, Lennon wrote *I Am the Walrus*, a song many consider to be one of his masterpieces. Four different inspirations have been identified for this song. Musically, Lennon said that he had been tinkering around on the piano when he happened to hear the sound of a police siren; he then attempted to incorporate its sound into a song. In contrast to his denials that the lyrics of *Lucy in the Sky with Diamonds* were influenced by LSD, Lennon openly admitted that the initial lines of *I Am the Walrus* were written while he was tripping on acid. Lennon also pointed once again to the influence of his favorite author, Lewis Carroll, as the song's title came from the poem "The Walrus and the Carpenter." Finally, Lennon said that he was imitating Bob Dylan's recent work:

Writing obscurely...never saying what you mean, but giving the *impression* of something. Where more *or* less can be read into it. It's a good game....Dylan got away with murder. I thought, Well, I can write this crap, too. You know, you just stick a few images together, thread them together, and you call it poetry (emphasis in original).

A full analysis of *I Am the Walrus* is clearly beyond the scope of the present book. Instead, I am concerned here with whether the song might represent an extension of the psychological processes that seem to have been unfolding when Lennon was writing *Lucy in the Sky with Diamonds*. Two intriguing parallels between the songs have already been mentioned: the influence of Lewis Carroll's poetry and of the drug LSD. Two musical similarities are also notable between *Lucy in the Sky with Diamonds* and *I Am the Walrus*: both begin in the key of A-major and portions of both songs are based on a sequence of chromatically descending chords. More remarkable still is the fact that the lyrics of *I Am the Walrus* have ten words in common with those of *Lucy in the Sky with Diamonds*: "climb(ing)," "down," "eye," "girl," "Lucy," "sky," "smile," "sun," "waiting," and "yellow." As such, *I Am the Walrus* shares twice the number of words with *Lucy in the Sky with Diamonds* as any song Lennon had written up to that point. Given the logic presented in chapter 4, it would seem likely that some kindred ideas were activated in Lennon's mind when he wrote each of these songs.

This possibility seems even greater given that the words "Lucy in the sky" are directly mentioned in the third verse of *I Am the Walrus*. There, Lennon sang:

Mister city policeman sitting pretty little policemen in a row
See how they fly like Lucy in the sky see how they run

Lennon suggested that his decision to include "policemen" in the first line of this stanza derived from the repetitive two-note police siren he had heard while sitting at the piano. Another biographer suggested that Lennon's combination of "policemen" with "Lucy in the sky" in this stanza is a reference to the "misinterpretation of *Lucy in the Sky with Diamonds* as a code for LSD." Perhaps these suggestions are correct. That said, one might still wonder whether Lennon had other associations to "policemen" that might have led him not only to mention them in *I Am the Walrus*, but to place them adjacent to "Lucy in the sky." Certainly he would have had common associations to "policemen" such as "law," "authority," and "arrest." At a more idiosyncratic level, however, "policemen" would likely have been part of Lennon's memories of Julia's death, as the person who informed the teen-aged Lennon of his mother's accident was a police officer, as was the man who drove the car that killed her.

This analysis might help explain the lines that immediately follow this lyrical collision between "policemen" and "Lucy." In the next four lines, Lennon sang that he is "crying," explicitly expressing the sadness that was absent from *Lucy in the Sky with Diamonds*. The next verse commences with a gruesome image of death derived from a rhyme Lennon heard as a boy on the playground:

Yellow matter custard, green slop pie
All mixed together with a dead dog's eye

Thus, in only a few lines composed of images that Lennon claimed were almost randomly stuck together, he mentioned a female stand-in for his mother (Lucy), sadness, death, and the "policemen" connected to both her death and his sadness.

That Lennon's thoughts about his childhood were quite active in the fall of 1967 is further suggested by the fact that not long after Epstein died, Lennon wrote a conciliatory letter to his father, Freddie, asking to see him again. Father and son had first been reunited in the spring of 1964 while the Beatles were filming *A Hard Day's Night*. They next encountered each other in February of 1966, when Freddie recorded a song (*That's My Life*) that Lennon felt was an exploitation of his own fame. As they argued over this issue, Freddie angered Lennon further by describing Julia's cheating ways and suggesting that she had abandoned the young Lennon to Mimi. In contrast to these earlier rocky reunions, conversations in the fall of 1967 between Freddie and Lennon went so well that Lennon invited his father to move in with him. Freddie stayed all of three weeks before moving out, as he was ignored by his busy son and bored living more or less alone in an enormous house.

Around the time when his father was temporarily back in his life, Lennon began working on another song, *Cry Baby Cry*. Here, for the very first time, Lennon explicitly used the word "mother" in the lyrics. And he did so both in the context of musical similarities to *Lucy in the Sky with Diamonds* (using the key of G-major and another descending chord progression) and in an explicit lyrical connection with sadness: "Cry baby cry, make your mother sigh" is repeated five times in the song. Death is also alluded to in the fourth verse where the children meet "for a séance in the dark." A séance, or the attempt to contact the spirit of a dead person, would have been among Lennon's memories of his mother's death. Nigel Walley (the friend who was with Julia moments before she was killed) told one of Lennon's biographers that a couple of months after Julia died, Lennon brought together several friends to hold a séance and try to reach her.

The First Half of 1968

As noted in chapter 6, fundamental to Bowlby's attachment theory is the idea that emotional distress results when people are separated from important individuals in their lives. Research studies consistently show this to be the case for infants, children, adolescents, and adults, and further document that the loneliness, anxiety, and depression that occur after separations are particularly intense for individuals who have anxious-ambivalent attachment styles. Such painful feelings are thought to be particularly severe for these individuals because separations in adulthood reactivate their beliefs that they desperately need relationships to soothe themselves but that other people are unlikely to be consistently available for that purpose.

Lennon experienced two noteworthy separations during the first half of 1968. First, Lennon's father moved to Scotland with his young fiancée (who had served briefly as Julian's nanny). Some stories suggest that this separation was precipitated by an argument between Lennon and Freddie about Lennon's wife Cynthia. In any case, although Lennon continued to send Freddie money, they once again parted, this time for almost three years.

The second, and certainly more crucial, separation was from Yoko Ono. Lennon first met this Japanese avant-garde artist in early November of 1966, previewing her show at a friend's art gallery and then seeing her again a couple of weeks later at another show. Soon after, Yoko sent Lennon her book of aphoristic poems, *Grapefruit*, which he kept by his bedside for months. Then sometime in the early part of 1967, Lennon invited her to lunch with him and Cynthia at their home to discuss the possibility of building a lighthouse Yoko had imaginatively described in her writings.

Accounts vary from this point. Some suggest that Lennon and Yoko had sex within three weeks of meeting, that Yoko often turned up at Lennon's home, and that she bombarded him with frequent notes stating things such as "Breathe" or "Watch the lights until dawn." Other accounts suggest that it was not until the fall of 1967 that Lennon attempted to seduce Yoko (when she refused, apparently). Certainly by then, however, they had interacted enough that Lennon was willing to provide the financial backing for one of her art shows, albeit anonymously.

What seems certain is that by early 1968 Lennon was deeply emotionally involved with Yoko. For example, one time when she returned to London after having traveled to Paris without telling him, Yoko found dozens of letters from Lennon awaiting her. And when Lennon was making plans to visit India in February of 1968 with Cynthia and the other Beatles, he initially invited Yoko to join his retinue before deciding that it was not feasible.

Lennon separated himself from Yoko to visit India at the behest of the Maharishi Mahesh Yogi, the founder of transcendental meditation. Lennon had first encountered the Maharishi in August of 1967, and had actually been at a retreat led by the guru when Epstein died. As the months passed, Lennon and the other Beatles remained interested in the possibilities of enlightenment, happiness, and peace promised by the process of losing one's ego through meditation. That February they fulfilled their promise to come study with the Maharishi at his ashram/resort in northern

India. Lennon stayed two months, hiding from Cynthia the fact that he was receiving almost daily letters from Yoko. Lennon later said of his time in India:

> I couldn't sleep and I was hallucinating like crazy—having dreams where you could smell. The funny thing about the camp was that although it was very beautiful and I was meditating about eight hours a day, I was writing the most miserable songs on earth. In *Yer Blues* when I wrote "I'm so lonely I want to die," (sic) I wasn't kidding. That's how I felt...up there, trying to reach God and feeling suicidal.

During the first part of 1968, Lennon continued his attempts to weaken his ego (now through meditation rather than LSD) and experienced separations both from his father and from Yoko, the woman with whom he was increasingly obsessed. Because these circumstances are the type that would heighten the accessibility of his thoughts and feelings about earlier separations in his life, it makes sense that "mothers" in general and, for the first time, Lennon's mother in particular, appeared in three of the songs that he began writing while in India.

In *The Continuing Story of Bungalow Bill*, Lennon satirized one of the meditators at the ashram who took a break from the peaceful vegetarian lifestyle at the ashram to go hunt tigers. As he had done in *Cry Baby Cry*, Lennon brought together children, mothers, and death in the last verse of this song:

> The children asked him if to kill was not a sin.
> "Not when he looked so fierce," his mommy butted in.

Yer Blues takes this progress even further. Although the song is typically described as Lennon's attempt to parody the "white blues" fad that was sweeping England in the late 1960s, a line like "Yes I'm lonely, wanna die" expressed well Lennon's experience of "feeling suicidal" while he was in India. In the context of these themes of loneliness, depression, and death, Lennon directly mentioned his own mother in the third verse: "My mother was of the sky." Not only does this line of *Yer Blues* connect "Lucy" and "my mother" via "sky," but it occurs at a critical musical juncture in the song. Recall that in *Lucy in the Sky with Diamonds* the time signature changes from 3/4 to 4/4; this transition happens between the lyrical phrase "and she's gone" and the repeated refrain "Lucy in the sky with diamonds." In *Yer Blues*, the underlying rhythm also seems to shift mid-song, in the very midst of the line "My mother was of the sky…"

Where *Yer Blues* pounds with pain and death, *Julia*, the other song which mentions his mother that Lennon started writing while he was in India, is soft, gentle, and comforting. But the musical and lyrical connections with *Lucy in the Sky with Diamonds* remain. For example, as he had done in the earlier song about Lucy, Lennon sang a repeated note multiple times in the first several measures of *Julia*. He also mentioned "Julia" in the context of many of the same images surrounding "Lucy," including the "sun," a "smile," a "cloud," and, most compellingly, "sky."

Late–1968 through Early–1970

Lennon and Cynthia returned from India in mid-April 1968, disillusioned after the Maharishi was accused of making sexual

come-ons to female meditators. No sooner were they reunited
with their son Julian than the family disbursed again: Lennon
to New York, Cynthia to Greece, and Julian to the home of the
housekeeper. Cynthia recalled:

> John was lying on our bed when I left. He was in the almost
> trance-like state I'd seen many times before and barely turned
> his head to say goodbye.

When Cynthia returned to her home in mid-May, it was to find
Lennon and Yoko sitting on the floor wearing bathrobes. Lennon
had invited Yoko over the night before, and the two worked
together recording the experimental music that would become
their first joint album, *Two Virgins*. Then they had sex and photo-
graphed themselves nude for what would become the cover of that
album. Cynthia recalled that when she walked in:

> John was facing me. He looked at me, expressionless, and
> said, "Oh, hi." Yoko didn't turn around...It was clear that
> they had arranged for me to find them like that and the
> cruelty of John's betrayal was hard to absorb. The intimacy
> between them was daunting. I could feel a wall round them
> that I could not penetrate.

Very soon after, Lennon left his wife and son; notably, Julian
was only several months younger than Lennon himself had been at
the time Freddie and Julia abandoned him as a boy.

Thus began a new phase of Lennon's adult life. Lennon and
Yoko soon began a series of art shows, experimental music concerts,

interviews while inside large bags, and the famous bed-ins for peace that would occupy them over the next several months and capture enormous media attention. Throughout, the two lovers were almost inseparable, with some claiming Yoko even regularly followed Lennon into the bathroom.

During the summer and fall of 1968, Yoko sat by Lennon's side as the Beatles recorded the songs they wrote in India that would form the basis for their next album, *The Beatles* (a.k.a., *The White Album*). Yoko's influence went far beyond her physical presence, however. On the avant-garde *Revolution 9*, she both helped in the mixing of the semi-random pastiche of sounds and spoke, "You become naked." Hers is also the female voice that speaks the part of the mother in *The Continuing Story of Bungalow Bill*, and she provided some of the inspiration for *Happiness is a Warm Gun*, as, according to Lennon, Yoko was the "Mother Superior" who would "jump the gun."

Yoko also seems to have helped with revisions of *Julia*, a song that Lennon said "was sort of a combination of Yoko and my mother blended into one." This merging of the two women is recognizable, for example, in Lennon's choice to refer to Julia as "ocean child," the transliteration of Yoko's name into English. Lennon's use of the images of "cloud" and "sky" might have referred on a subconscious level not only to Lucy/Julia, but also to Yoko, who had sent him a card while he was in India saying that she was a cloud who could be found in the sky. Perhaps the merging of Yoko and Julia allowed Lennon to express more explicitly his positive emotions about his mother; after all, while Lucy "calls you," Julia "calls me."

As these examples attest, Lennon took multiple opportunities to psychologically identify Yoko with, or perhaps even as, his mother. During this early stage of their relationship, Yoko also provided Lennon with the constant presence and opportunity to merge with someone that he seems to have yearned for since experiencing the inconsistent parenting he received from Julia during his infancy, her abandonment of him, and her death. Put in the parlance of attachment theory, Yoko Ono met Lennon's attachment needs in a way no woman had previously.

Yoko also seems to have been involved with Lennon's switch in drug of choice from LSD to heroin. As with other elements of his life, biographers disagree about whether Lennon had tried heroin before his relationship with Yoko became serious, but it is clear that by the fall of 1968 the two of them were regularly using the drug and would continue to do so for at least the next year, and probably a bit longer. It would be difficult to find a drug with psychological effects more different from LSD. By its nature, heroin is an opiate and acts to ease pain. After injecting or inhaling it, an almost immediate rush of ecstasy washes over one's whole body and mind, a pleasure many users claim is more intense than an orgasm. Soon after, one goes "on the nod," lying for hours in a state of what has been called "blissful apathy." In contrast to the deep spiritual and personal awakenings that many experience while on LSD, heroin numbs one with pleasure. And for people like Lennon and Yoko, who had enough money and personal aides to keep them constantly supplied, it was relatively easy to remain in what Lennon later characterized as a "strange cocktail of love, sex, and forgetfulness," where he felt "like a baby wrapped in cotton wool and floating in warm water."

Compared to early 1967 through mid-1968, therefore, the conditions of Lennon's life from mid-1968 through early 1970 would have likely diminished the accessibility of his thoughts and feelings about his mother and her death. Between frequently drugging himself into a state of "blissful apathy" and having gained close and constant contact with a female who happily obliged his desires for union, Lennon seems to have experienced a respite from the painful thoughts and feelings that in the previous months had been slowly working their way from the periphery to the center of his awareness. Perhaps this explains why after writing a string of songs in which his feelings about Julia had become increasingly (though still incompletely) expressed, Lennon wrote zero songs between late-1968 and early-1970 that explicitly mentioned Lucy, mothers, or his own mother.

9 | EXPRESSION

I n the fall of 1970, Lennon once again opened the door on the expression of his feelings about his mother and her death. Indeed, he knocked the door completely off its hinges.

Earlier that spring, the Beatles had officially disbanded and Lennon was once again forced to confront the question of how he would construct a new life for himself. Yoko had also recently suffered two miscarriages, the second rather late into her pregnancy. And around this same time, Lennon seems to have drastically reduced his heroin intake. The combination of another separation (from the Beatles), two more deaths (of his potential children), and the relative cessation of his self-medication (with heroin) might explain Lennon's reaction that March when he received in the mail an advance copy of the book *Primal Scream: Primal Therapy, the Cure for Neurosis*. Lennon immediately read the entire book, in which the American psychotherapist Arthur Janov presented his extension and elaboration of Freud's ideas that psychological suffering could be relieved through the strong emotional release (or catharsis) of the pain people carry around from their childhood.

Upon finishing the book, Lennon contacted Janov, asking the therapist to come to England and begin treating him. Janov agreed, and the two worked together almost daily that spring and summer, first at Lennon's home in England and then at Janov's therapy center in Los Angeles. Janov later described Lennon's pain as "enormous...as much as I've ever seen...He had no defenses...he was just one big ball of pain." Over the weeks the two talked at length about Lennon's childhood abandonments, the numerous people who had "died on him," and his angry, tender, and sometimes incestuous feelings towards his mother. Throughout, Janov encouraged Lennon to literally scream, cry, and rage about his sadness, anger, and despair. Lennon came to learn that:

> My defenses were so great. I mean the cocky chip-on-the-shoulder, macho, aggressive rock-and-roll hero who knew all the answers and the smart quip, the sharp-talking king of the world was actually a terrified guy who didn't know how to cry. Simple. Now I can cry. That's what I learned from primal therapy.

And:

> Instead of penting up emotion or pain, feel it rather than putting it away for some rainy day.... It's like somewhere along the line, we were switched off not to feel things.... This therapy gives you back the switch, locate it and switch back into feeling just as a human being, not as a male or female or a famous person or not famous person, they switch you back to being a baby and therefore you feel as a child does.

Despite Janov's warning that therapy should continue for months longer, Lennon was forced to leave Los Angeles that September, as his US visa had expired. Fueled by his experience of primal therapy that summer and by a tongue-lashing he applied to his father that October, Lennon began writing songs that autumn that no longer hid his feelings behind the Lewis Carroll allusions and the wild and seemingly disconnected hallucinogenic imagery that had so obfuscated the meanings of *Lucy in the Sky with Diamonds* and many other songs. Instead, Lennon began recording songs that expressed in simple, forceful, and emotionally harrowing ways the feelings he had long carried around about his childhood, his father, and his mother.

These songs appeared on his first post-Beatles studio album, *John Lennon/Plastic Ono Band*. The first song on the album is *Mother*, where Lennon sang to Julia, "I wanted you, you didn't want me," and at the end of the song incanted, "Mama don't go" ten times in ever-increasing wails and screams. Notably, the longest wails occur on the word "go," which, grammatically speaking, is the base form of the word "gone" that Lennon had used in *Lucy in the Sky with Diamonds* to describe Lucy's disappearance.

Then, in two very angry songs, Lennon directly referred to the pain of his abandonments. In *I Found Out* he snarled:

> I heard something 'bout my Ma and my Pa
> They didn't want me so they made me a star...

And in *Working Class Hero* he accuses adults of:

> giving you no time instead of it all
> 'Til the pain is so big you feel nothing at all

The album closes with *My Mummy's Dead*, a short, simple, and emotionally devastating song intoned in what one biographer aptly described as "the voice of a dazed child." Amidst repetitions of the title phrase, Lennon bemoans how his mother's death caused "so much pain" that he could "never show."

In these songs written for *John Lennon/Plastic Ono Band*, Lennon's pain is obvious, his past attempts to suppress his pain are acknowledged, and the events that caused "so much pain" are explicitly described. There is almost no need for the psychobiographical methods that were required to decipher and decode *Lucy in the Sky with Diamonds,* for by the fall of 1970 Lennon had become able to express fully his feelings about his childhood, his mother, and her death. Rather than using the kind of emotionally distanced linguistic devices that so characterized *Lucy in the Sky with Diamonds*, Lennon now wrote his songs in an emotionally immediate way: most of the words are short, the pronouns are primarily first person singular, the verbs are mostly in the present tense, and the negative affect is prominent. In these songs Lennon also relied less and less on the lyrical and musical idioms that had characterized *Lucy in the Sky with Diamonds* and the other songs he had written that skirted around the issues of loss, death, depression, and his mother. The songs on *Plastic Ono Band* contain no mother up in the sky, none of the idealized imagery that surrounded her in *Julia*, and no veiled allusions to sadness and death connected only by chains of associations. These songs also have little in the way of the complex time changes and chord progressions that were present in earlier songs. Indeed, about the only striking musical similarity between *Lucy in the Sky with Diamonds* and the songs on *John Lennon/Plastic Ono Band* is Lennon's use of the repeated three-note descent around which the melody of *My Mummy's Dead* is based.

Although the style, words, and music shifted as Lennon came to express his feelings rather than defend against them, the fundamental script that characterized *Lucy in the Sky with Diamonds* remains clearly present in these songs from *Plastic Ono Band*: There is a powerful female with whom Lennon wanted to be close, but she would not stay near him. By the fall of 1970, Lennon could plainly reveal these feelings, both to himself and to others, for what they had always been.

AFTERWORD

So many interesting questions about Lennon remain to be answered.

For example, is it the case that venting some of the pain from his past later helped Lennon to write optimistic songs like *Imagine* and happy songs like *Oh Yoko* on the 1971 *Imagine* album? Might it be that his primal screams exorcised the daemon/muse that had propelled his creativity for so many years, leading Lennon to release albums after *Imagine* that many critics and fans viewed as substantially weaker than his earlier efforts? Was the drug and alcohol binge Lennon went on in 1974 (i.e., "The Lost Weekend") the result of his anxious-ambivalent attachment style rising to the fore after Yoko kicked him out of their home? Did Lennon's efforts to come to grips with his parents play any role in his decision to retire from music when his second son, Sean, was born in 1975? Were Lennon's songs on the 1980 *Double Fantasy* album reflective of a successful resolution of the problems from earlier in his life?

I am of course tempted to try to answer these and other questions, as I believe that some light could be shed on them by examining the features of Lennon's personality examined in this book. Old habits and beliefs are very rarely, if ever, extracted like a rotten tooth from one's psyche, and what one first learned tends to persist in one's mind, even as one learns new, sometimes contradictory, information. Thus, even though Lennon's personality may have begun to shift in some important ways by late 1970, the beliefs and coping strategies he had come to hold as a result of the painful facts of his childhood and adolescence were unlikely to have changed so much in the last decade of his life as to render them completely irrelevant.

But as I hope readers who have come this far will appreciate, the overall approach that I have utilized throughout this book suggests that it would be both presumptuous and overly reductionistic to assume that convincing answers to questions about Lennon's later life could be obtained primarily by examining the facts of Lennon's childhood and adolescence. Such information is just not enough. Answering new questions in a psychologically compelling manner would necessitate a deep, multifaceted analysis of whatever songs or events one was trying to explain. As such, wholly new sets of Linguistic Inquiry and Word Count, scripting, and association analyses would need to be conducted on the later songs that are especially relevant to those other questions. Further, it may be that answering some of these questions (e.g., about Lennon's retirement) would benefit from the development of new methodological approaches that are less song-dependent.

I also hope readers will remember from chapters 6 and 7 that a full explanation of why Lennon wrote *Lucy in the Sky with Diamonds* in the way he did, at the time he did, required not only an exposition of his personal history (e.g., his attachment and coping styles) but also inspection of his "recent past" (e.g., his stresses and LSD use) and of the event that "activated" the composition (i.e., Julian's picture). Further, the analyses presented in chapters 8 and 9 suggest that the extent to which Lennon continued to express his thoughts and feelings about his mother depended in large part on the circumstances of his life (e.g., the drugs he was taking, the deaths he had experienced). If *Lucy in the Sky with Diamonds* was indeed the result of a coalescence of his personal history, his experiences in the months of 1966 and early 1967, and the specific activating event of being handed a particular picture by his son, then it is extremely likely that *any* later songs he wrote or decisions he made would also be due to the joint interaction of his personal history, relevant recent developments in his life, and specific catalytic events.

For all of these reasons, while I have found it an interesting and eye-opening challenge to analyze *Lucy in the Sky with Diamonds* and its place in Lennon's life, it seems to me that attempts to answer other questions about Lennon are best reserved for future psychobiographies that can explore these questions with the full attention that they deserve.

Comparison Songs Used in Linguistic Inquiry and Word Count Analyses

Sample 1: Recent John Lennon Songs
A Day in the Life (from *Sgt. Pepper's Lonely Hearts Club Band*; McCartney's middle portion omitted)
And Your Bird Can Sing (from *Revolver*)
Being for the Benefit of Mr. Kite (from *Sgt. Pepper's Lonely Hearts Club Band*)
Doctor Robert (from *Revolver*)
Good Morning Good Morning (from *Sgt. Pepper's Lonely Hearts Club Band*)
I'm Only Sleeping (from *Revolver*)
Rain (from *Revolver*)
She Said She Said (from *Revolver*)
Strawberry Fields Forever (Single)
Tomorrow Never Knows (from *Revolver*)

(*Continued*)

Sample 2: No. 1 US and UK Hit Singles between January 1, 1966 and mid-February, 1967

96 Tears—? & the Mysterians—US
All or Nothing—The Small Faces—UK
Cherish—The Association—US
Distant Drums—Jim Reeves—UK
Get Away—Georgie Fame and The Blue Flames—UK
Good Lovin'—The Young Rascals—US
Good Vibrations—The Beach Boys—US and UK
Green Green Grass of Home—Tom Jones—UK
Hanky Panky—Tommy James—US
I'm a Believer—The Monkees—US and UK
Keep on Running—The Spencer Davis Group—UK
Kind of a Drag—The Buckinghams—US
Last Train to Clarksville—The Monkees—US
Lightnin' Strikes—Lou Christie—US
Monday, Monday—The Mamas & The Papas—US
My Love—Petula Clark—US
Out of Time—Chris Farlowe—UK
Paint It Black—Rolling Stones—US and UK
Poor Side of Town—Johnny Rivers—US
Pretty Flamingo—Manfred Mann—UK
Reach Out I'll Be There—The Four Tops—US and UK
Somebody Help Me—The Spencer Davis Group—UK
Strangers in the Night—Frank Sinatra—US and UK
Summer in the City—The Lovin' Spoonful—US
Sunny Afternoon—The Kinks—UK

(*Continued*)

Sample 2: No. I US and UK Hit Singles between January 1, 1966 and mid-February, 1967
Sunshine Superman—Donovan—US
The Ballad of the Green Berets—Sgt. Barry Sadler—US
The Sound of Silence—Simon & Garfunkel—US
The Sun Ain't Gonna Shine Anymore—The Walker Brothers—UK
These Boots Are Made for Walking—Nancy Sinatra—US and UK
This is My Song—Petula Clark—UK
When a Man Loves a Woman—Percy Sledge—US
Wild Thing—The Troggs—US
Winchester Cathedral—The New Vaudeville Band—US
With a Girl Like You—The Troggs—UK
You Can't Hurry Love—The Supremes—US
You Don't Have to Say You Love Me—Dusty Springfield—UK
You Keep Me Hangin' On—The Supremes—US
(You're My) Soul and Inspiration—The Righteous Brothers—US

Note: The list of songs for Sample 2 comes from: http://www.wwwk.co.uk/music/hit-singles/years/1966.htm; http://www.wwwk.co.uk/music/hit-singles/years/1967.htm; and http://www.popculturemadness.com/Music/Number-One-Songs-60s.html. I omitted the following no. 1 songs from Sample 2 because they were written and/or performed by the Beatles: *Michelle* (covered by the Overlanders, UK), *Paperback Writer* (US and UK), *We Can Work It Out* (US), and *Yellow Submarine/Eleanor Rigby* (UK).

APPENDIX B

Statistical Comparisons of Linguistic Inquiry and Word Count (LIWC) Results for *Lucy in the Sky with Diamonds* Compared to Songs Lennon had Written in the Previous Months

LIWC Indicator	LSD % of Words	Mean % of Words in Recent Lennon Songs	Standard Deviation of Recent Lennon Songs	LSD's Z-Score
>6 letters	20.35	11.03	7.02	1.33
Pronouns	6.19	18.62	10.27	−1.22
First person singular	0.00	6.38	6.14	−1.04
First person plural	0.00	0.00	0.00	n/a
Second person	3.10	4.93	5.30	−0.34
Third person singular	1.33	1.33	1.65	0.00
Third person plural	0.00	0.68	1.26	−0.54
Articles	13.72	6.87	5.06	1.35
Verbs	3.98	19.64	9.16	−1.71
Past tense verbs	0.88	2.73	4.22	−0.44
Present tense verbs	3.10	13.60	7.27	−1.44
Future tense verbs	0.00	1.36	1.82	−0.75

(*Continued*)

LIWC Indicator	LSD % of Words	Mean % of Words in Recent Lennon Songs	Standard Deviation of Recent Lennon Songs	LSD's Z-Score
Adverbs	1.77	4.41	3.41	−0.77
Prepositions	24.78	11.04	5.87	2.34
Conjunctions	2.65	5.56	3.55	−0.82
Negaters	0.00	3.28	2.28	−1.44
Numbers	0.00	0.60	0.78	−0.77
Social	7.96	12.55	7.98	−0.58
Family	0.00	0.07	0.23	−0.30
Friend	0.00	0.22	0.73	−0.30
Humans	1.77	1.29	1.73	0.27
Affect	0.44	5.89	6.12	−0.89
Positive emotion	0.44	4.72	6.34	−0.68
Negative Emotion	0.00	1.17	1.18	−0.99
Cognitive	14.60	13.75	4.87	0.17
Insight	0.44	2.86	3.08	−0.79
Cause	0.00	0.96	1.15	−0.83
Discrepancy	0.00	0.83	0.85	−0.98
Tentative	1.77	1.42	0.88	0.39
Certainty	0.00	2.28	2.32	−0.99
Inhibition	0.44	0.30	0.53	0.26
Inclusive	11.95	3.50	3.11	2.72
Exclusive	0.00	2.08	1.89	−1.10
Perceptual	3.98	4.58	3.04	−0.20
Seeing	3.98	2.20	2.17	0.82
Hearing	0.00	1.79	2.02	−0.89
Feeling	0.00	0.87	0.98	−0.89

(*Continued*)

LIWC Indicator	LSD % of Words	Mean % of Words in Recent Lennon Songs	Standard Deviation of Recent Lennon Songs	LSD's Z-Score
Biology	2.65	2.94	3.68	−0.08
Body	2.21	1.11	2.14	0.51
Health	0.00	1.36	3.22	−0.42
Sexual	0.00	0.27	0.60	−0.45
Ingestion	0.44	0.20	0.29	0.84
Relativity	26.11	15.46	8.45	1.26
Motion	3.98	2.15	1.54	1.19
Space	19.91	6.59	5.56	2.40
Time	2.21	6.50	4.52	−0.95
Work	0.00	1.71	3.64	−0.47
Achievement	0.44	0.79	1.05	−0.33
Leisure	0.00	1.76	1.49	−1.18
Home	0.00	0.30	0.68	−0.44
Money	0.00	0.17	0.39	−0.42
Religion	0.00	0.17	0.41	−0.42
Death	0.00	0.64	1.14	−0.56

Note: The first column reports the Linguistic Inquiry and Word Count (LIWC) indicator. The second column reports the percentage of words in *Lucy in the Sky with Diamonds* that score positively for selected LIWC indicators. The third column reports the *mean*, or the statistical average, of the percentage of words in the 11 songs in the sample, including *Lucy in the Sky with Diamonds*. The fourth column reports the *standard deviation* for each indicator in this sample; standard deviations are measures of the extent to which scores in the sample deviate from the mean, with high numbers indicating greater dispersal. The fifth column reports the *z-score*, which is calculated by subtracting the sample mean from *Lucy in the Sky with Diamonds'* score and then dividing the resulting number by the standard deviation. Positive z-scores indicate how far the score for *Lucy in the Sky with Diamonds* is above the sample mean, whereas negative z-scores indicate how far the score for *Lucy in the Sky with Diamonds* is below the sample mean. The larger the absolute value of the z-score, the more different *Lucy in the Sky with Diamonds* is from the other songs in the sample. A z-score could not be calculated for first person plural pronouns because the standard deviation was 0 for the sample.

Statistical Comparisons of Linguistic Inquiry and Word
Count (LIWC) Results for *Lucy in the Sky with Diamonds*
Compared to No. 1 Us and Uk Hit Singles between
January 1, 1966 and Mid-February 1967

LIWC Indicator	*LSD*% of Words	Mean % of Words in Recent Hit Songs	Standard Deviation of Recent Hit Songs	*LSD's* Z-score
> 6 letters	20.35	9.40	4.67	2.39
Pronouns	6.19	20.27	8.03	−1.74
First person singular	0.00	8.55	5.23	−1.63
First person plural	0.00	0.56	1.03	−0.55
Second person	3.10	5.16	4.51	−0.45
Third person singular	1.33	1.40	2.76	−0.02
Third person plural	0.00	0.31	0.64	−0.48
Articles	13.72	5.19	4.14	2.09
Verbs	3.98	19.69	7.01	−2.24

(*Continued*)

LIWC Indicator	LSD% of Words	Mean % of Words in Recent Hit Songs	Standard Deviation of Recent Hit Songs	LSD's Z-score
Past tense verbs	0.88	2.85	2.82	−0.70
Present tense verbs	3.10	13.18	5.55	−1.81
Future tense verbs	0.00	2.10	1.98	−1.06
Adverbs	1.77	5.12	2.93	−1.13
Prepositions	24.78	10.61	5.10	2.73
Conjunctions	2.65	5.01	2.54	−0.92
Negaters	0.00	3.19	3.47	−0.92
Numbers	0.00	0.86	1.48	−0.58
Social	7.96	15.17	8.16	−0.87
Family	0.00	0.10	0.37	−0.26
Friend	0.00	0.14	0.32	−0.45
Humans	1.77	2.43	3.93	−0.17
Affect	0.44	6.84	5.70	−1.12
Positive emotion	0.44	5.20	5.34	−0.89
Negative Emotion	0.00	1.64	3.23	−0.51
Cognitive	14.60	15.99	5.91	−0.29
Insight	0.44	1.99	1.83	−0.84
Cause	0.00	1.68	1.73	−0.97
Discrepancy	0.00	1.82	1.80	−1.01
Tentative	1.77	1.95	2.57	−0.06
Certainty	0.00	2.24	1.81	−1.24
Inhibition	0.44	1.13	1.73	−0.39
Inclusive	11.95	3.75	2.94	2.67
Exclusive	0.00	2.58	2.00	−1.29

(Continued)

LIWC Indicator	LSD% of Words	Mean % of Words in Recent Hit Songs	Standard Deviation of Recent Hit Songs	LSD's Z-score
Perceptual	3.98	4.15	2.95	−0.04
Seeing	3.98	1.71	2.07	1.12
Hearing	0.00	1.26	1.98	−0.63
Feeling	0.00	1.04	1.24	−0.84
Biology	2.65	2.75	2.10	−0.04
Body	2.21	1.07	1.06	1.09
Health	0.00	0.36	0.76	−0.47
Sexual	0.00	1.31	1.83	−0.72
Ingestion	0.44	0.07	0.31	1.22
Relativity	26.11	16.00	8.00	1.18
Motion	3.98	2.42	1.80	0.89
Space	19.91	7.04	5.13	2.46
Time	2.21	6.06	5.49	−0.78
Work	0.00	0.25	0.63	−0.39
Achievement	0.44	0.53	0.89	−0.09
Leisure	0.00	0.88	1.22	−0.72
Home	0.00	0.23	0.65	−0.36
Money	0.00	0.24	0.55	−0.44
Religion	0.00	0.18	0.51	−0.35
Death	0.00	0.10	0.29	−0.34

Note: See note in appendix B. The only difference for this table is that the means, standard deviations, and z-scores are based on the sample of recent popular songs (including *Lucy in the Sky with Diamonds*), rather than recent Lennon songs.

Results of Association Analysis for the 22 Words
that Appeared in *Lucy in the Sky with Diamonds* and in
Songs Lennon had Previously Written

Word	Place in the Earlier Song Where the Word Appeared	Associations to the Word in the Earlier Song
Appear	Refrain—I'm a Loser	Hiding (feelings)
Away	Verse 2—Anytime at All	Comfort (given)
	Verse 3—A Day in the Life	Separation (ignored)
	Verse 2—I'm Only Sleeping	Hiding
	Verse 1—Ticket to Ride	Separation (loss)
	Refrain—You've Got to Hide Your Love Away	Hiding (feelings)
Call(s)	Verses 1, 3, Refrain—All I've Got to Do	Comfort (given and received)
	Refrain, Verses 1, 2—Anytime at All	Comfort (given)
	Verse 1—Doctor Robert	Comfort (received)
	Verse 1—Good Morning, Good Morning	Death
	Verses 1, 2, Fade Out—I Call Your Name	Separation (abandoned)
Diamonds	Verse 3—I Feel Fine	Love (has)
Down	Verses 1, 2 of Bridge—And Your Bird Can Sing	Burden; Sadness
	Verse 2—Doctor Robert	Sadness; Comfort (received)
	Bridge—Girl	Insulting relationship
	Verse 2—Good Morning, Good Morning	Sadness
	Refrain—Help!	Sadness; Comfort (desired)
	Verse 2—It Won't Be Long	Sadness
	Refrain—Strawberry Fields Forever	Sharing information
	Verse 2—Ticket to Ride	Insulting relationship; Sadness
	Verses 1, 2—You Can't Do That	Jealousy; Separation (ending relationship)

(Continued)

Eyes	Verse 1—*Anytime at All*	Love (desired)
	Verse 2—*Hello Little Girl*	Love (desired)
	Bridge—*I'm Only Sleeping*	Observing
	Verse 2—*It Won't be Long*	Sadness
	Verse 1—*Strawberry Fields Forever*	Hiding (from external world)
Flowers	Verse 1 of Bridge—*Hello Little Girl*	Separation (rejection)
Girl	Verse 1, Refrain, Bridge—*Girl*	Insulting Relationship
	Verses 1, 2, Fade Out—*Hello Little Girl*	Love (desires)
	Bridge—*I Feel Fine*	Love (has)
	Verse 1—*I Should Have Known Better*	Love (has)
	Verse 1—*I'll Cry Instead*	Separation (loss)
	Verse 1—*I'm a Loser*	Separation (loss)
	Verse 1—*Norwegian Wood*	Love (has)
	Verse 1—*Please Please Me*	Conflict in relationship
	Verse 1, Refrain—*Run for Your Life*	Death; Jealousy; Hiding (self)
	Verse 1—*Ticket to Ride*	Separation (loss)
	Verse 2—*When I Get Home*	Love (has)
	Refrain—*You're Going to Lose That Girl*	Separation (loss)

(Continued)

Word	Place in the Earlier Song Where the Word Appeared	Associations to the Word in the Earlier Song
Gone	Verses 1, 3—*Help!*	Sadness
	Verse 1—*I Call Your Name*	Separation (loss)
	Verses 1, 3—*I Don't Want to Spoil the Party*	Separation (abandoned)
	Verse 1—*In My Life*	Change
	Verse 2—*You're Going to Lose That Girl*	Separation (loss)
	Verse 1—*You've Got to Hide Your Love Away*	Separation (loss); Sadness
Green	Verse 2—*And Your Bird Can Sing*	Hiding (self)
	Bridge—*You Can't Do That*	Jealousy
Head	Verse 1—*Being for the Benefit of Mr. Kite*	Challenge
	Verses 1, 4—*I'm Only Sleeping*	Awakening
	Verse 1—*Rain*	Hiding (self); Death
	Verse 1, Refrain—*Run for Your Life*	Hiding (self); Jealousy; Death
	Verse 2—*She Said She Said*	Death; Sadness; Insanity
	Verse 1—*You've Got to Hide Your Love Away*	Separation (loss); Sadness
High	Verse 1—*It's Only Love*	Love (has)
	Verse 2—*Strawberry Fields Forever*	Separation (alone)
	Bridge—*Ticket to Ride*	Separation (loss)

(Continued)

Look	Bridge—*And Your Bird Can Sing*	Comfort (given)
	Verse 1—*Anytime at All*	Love (desired)
	Verse 3—*A Day in the Life*	Desire to know
	Bridge—*Girl*	Insulting relationship
	Verses 1, 3—*I Don't Want to Spoil the Party*	Separation (abandoned)
	Verse 1—*No Reply*	Jealousy
	Bridge—*Norwegian Wood*	Lack of physical comfort
People	Verses 2, 3—*A Day in the Life*	Being the center of attention;
		Separation (ignored)
		Rushing
	Bridge—*Good Morning, Good Morning*	Separation (self-imposed); Hiding (feelings)
	Verse 2, Bridge—*I'll Cry Instead*	Love (has)
	Verse 2—*In My Life*	Being the center of attention; Being judged
	Verse 1—*You've Got to Hide Your Love Away*	
Sky	Verse 2—*I'm a Loser*	Separation (loss); Sadness
Smile	Verse 2—*Good Morning, Good Morning*	Elation
Somebody	Verse 1—*Anytime at All*	Love (desired)
	Verse 3—*Good Morning, Good Morning*	Comfort (given)
	Intro—*Help!*	Comfort (desired)
	Verse 2—*Nowhere Man*	Comfort (received)

(*Continued*)

Word	Place in the Earlier Song Where the Word Appeared	Associations to the Word in the Earlier Song
Someone	Intro—*Help!*	Comfort (desired)
	Refrain—*I'm a Loser*	Separation (loss)
	Verse 1—*Little Child*	Love (desired)
Station	Bridge—*One After 909*	Separation (abandoned)
Sun	Verse 2—*Anytime at All*	Comfort (given)
	Verse 2—*Rain*	Relaxing
Take	Bridge—*Baby's in Black*	Sadness
	Bridge—*I Call Your Name*	Sadness
	Verse 2—*I Don't Want to Spoil the Party*	Separation (abandoned)
	Verse 2—*Nowhere Man*	Rushing
	Refrain—*Strawberry Fields Forever*	Sharing information
Tree	Verse 2—*Strawberry Fields Forever*	Separation (alone)

Note: "Refrain" refers to the main chorus of the song. "Verses" refers to lyrics that go along with a repeated melodic motif that is not the refrain. "Bridge" refers to an eight-, four-, or even two-bar portion of the song that separates verses from each other (or from the refrain) and that has a different melodic motif than either the refrain or the verses. "Intro" refers to the very beginning of the song. "Fade out" refers to the portion of the song that is repeated at its end.

Most Common Free Associations of College Students to Words that Appear Both in *Lucy in the Sky with Diamonds* and in Songs Lennon had Previously Written

Appear	disappear, see, seem, look, show, come, present, there, vanish, become, happen, here, hide, leave, stage
Away	gone, home, here, near, close, from, stay, go, leave, vacation, come, school, together, college, goodbye, trip
Call	phone, telephone, answer, yell, collect, talk, wait, dial, girl, holler, listen, mom, need, ring
Diamonds	ring, gold, emerald, sparkle, big, expensive, money, pearl, earring, engagement, gem, girl, jewel, necklace, rich, rock, ruby
Down	up, under, town, low, elevator, fall, out, depressed, descend, lower
Eyes	blue, nose, ears, face, see, sight, color, glasses, lashes, pupils, black, brown, head, pretty, vision
Flowers	roses, pretty, beautiful, bouquet, petals, smell, daisies, bloom, colors, plant, happiness, scent, bright, garden, love, nature, spring, trees, vase, wonderful
Girl	boy, friend, woman, pretty, female, guy, innocence, lady
Gone	left, away, wind, went, here, disappear, leave, bye, forever, goodbye, come, lost, our, back, dead, dust, going, long, mad, return

(*Continued*)

Green	grass, yellow, blue, color, red, leaf, arrow, clover, frog, vegetables, apple, bean, elf, go, money, nature, tree
Head	hair, ache, brain, toe, tail, face, feet, body, hat, neck, pot, top, shop, shoulder, think
High	low, mountain, up, drug, tall, fly, kite, plane, rise, school, sky
Look	see, eye, watch, out, listen, stare, glance, gaze, magazine, observe, read
People	crowd, person, friend, place, different, group, human, family, animal, city, many, nice, population, associate, like, mix, strange, world
Sky	blue, cloud, sun, heaven, air, high, ground, plane, skydiving, space, star, up
Smile	happy, frown, laugh, teeth, face, grin, friendly, happiness, love, beautiful, mouth, pretty
Somebody	No norms available
Someone	No norms available
Station	train, gas, radio, wagon, railroad, bus, channel, depot, place, television
Sun	tan, moon, hot, shine, warm, beach, fun, heat, burn, bright, light, Florida, rays, star
Take	give, steal, receive, get, away, grab, have, home, obtain, leave, selfish
Tree	leaf, trunk, house, climb, green, stump, oak, shade, bush, forest, bark, branch, top, cat, flower, fort, limb, nature, pine, squirrel, tall

Note: These associations are based on studies in which participants were presented with a target word (in the first column) and asked to write down the first word that came to mind. The words listed in the second column are presented in descending order of the frequency with which they were given in response to the target word. More information about the method and these associations can be found in appendix A of the University of South Florida's Free Association Norms, accessible at: http://w3.usf.edu/FreeAssociation/.

Musical Similarities between *Lucy in the Sky with Diamonds*, *Help!*, and *Strawberry Fields Forever*

Feature of Lucy in the Sky with Diamonds	Similarity in *Help!*	Similarity in *Strawberry Fields Forever*
Time Change	None	4/4 to 2/4 to 3/4 to 4/4 when singing refrain, (e.g. measures 11–14; 29–32, 48–51)
Key Signature in A-major, B-flat-major, or G-major	A-major	A-major/B-flat-major (See Notes on the Methods)
Key Change	See Notes on the Methods	See Notes on the Methods
Three-note stepwise descent in melody	Ending of the song's introduction (measure 7); specific words in measures 11, 20, 27, 31, 43, 52, 59, 63, 75, 84, 91, and 95; and twice at the end of the refrain in measures 37–38, 69–70, and 101–102.	None

(*Continued*)

Feature of Lucy in the Sky with Diamonds	Similarity in *Help!*	Similarity in *Strawberry Fields Forever*
Repeating note in melody	First measures (9–11, 41–43, 73–75) and middle measures (17–19, 49–51, 81–83) of each verse	First two measures of each verse (e.g., measures 15–16, 34–35, and 53–54)
Chord progression with stepwise descent	B, A, G, F-sharp, E at introduction of song (measures 1–6) and in the refrain (measures 25–36, 57–68, and 89–100)	E, D-sharp, D, C-sharp at introduction (measures 1–3) and in the first two measures of each verse (i.e., measures 15–16, 34–35, and 53–54)

Notes: Measures enumerated in this table refer to versions of the songs transcribed by Lowry (1988). Neither *Help!* nor *Strawberry Fields Forever* began in 3/4 time or used the long, descending melodic theme, so these two characteristics are not listed in appendix F. See Notes on the Methods regarding my decision process concerning key and key change.

NOTES ON THE TEXT

As with the other books in this series on psychobiography, I chose not to
  clutter the text with citations and references. The prose below describes
  the particular references that informed my analysis, the specific studies,
  anecdotes, and theories referred to, and the sources for most quotes.

OPENING QUOTATIONS

The first two quotations are from Giuliano & Giuliano (1996, pp. 106 and
  145). The third quote is from Sheff (2000, p. 176) and is reprinted by
  permission of St. Martin's Press.

CHAPTER 1

The quote in which Lennon denies that *Lucy in the Sky with Diamonds* is
  about LSD comes from Sheff (2000, p. 182) and is reprinted by permission
  of St. Martin's Press.

The story of the drawing and the Carroll poem that came to Lennon's mind is
  repeated by numerous biographers, including Everett (1999, pp. 103–105)
  and Lennon (2005, p. 194). Julian's drawing can be seen on the cover of his
  2009 EP, *Lucy*.

The quote in which Lennon says that Lucy is the "imaginary girl that we all
  have" comes from Sheff (2000, pp. 181–182) and is reprinted by permission
  of St. Martin's Press.

MacDonald's (1994) speculation can be found in footnote 2 on p. 191.

Debates about the meaning of *Lucy in the Sky with Diamonds* continue even
  four decades after the song was released. For example, of the 500,000-plus
  lyrics available for discussion on http://www.songmeanings.net, *Lucy in
  the Sky with Diamonds* was the 67th most discussed song at this writing
  (in the summer of 2010). It was also the only song from the decade of the
  1960s that was among the 100 most commented-upon songs (Schiano,

personal communication, August 8, 2010). Many of the 443 comments made about the song between 2002 and the summer of 2010 either claim that Lennon and the other Beatles were lying—since the song is obviously about an LSD experience—or remind the website's visitors about the story of Julian's drawing.

See MacDonald (1994) for analyses of *Day Tripper* (pp. 133–135) and *Tomorrow Never Knows* (pp. 148–153).

Evidence that St. Louis has an over-representation of people named Louis and dentists have an over-representation of people named Dennis comes from Pelham, Mirenberg, & Jones (2002).

These and other definitions for the acronym LSD can be found at: http://acronyms.thefreedictionary.com/lsd.

That Julian painted "endless pictures for Daddy" is attested to by Cynthia Lennon (2005, p. 170); the quote is reprinted by permission of Random House, Inc.

See Goldman (1988) or Norman (2008) regarding the chronology of Lennon and Yoko Ono's early interactions.

The quote by Spignesi & Lewis (2004) is on p. 50 of their book.

Alexander (1990, pp. 13–24) provides the full list of rules to consider.

CHAPTER 2

The contrast between these poems of Plath's and Sexton's was first discussed by Pennebaker & Stone (2004). See Stirman & Pennebaker (2001) for more on suicidality and linguistic style among poets. The poems can be found in Levertov (1964) and the biographical note to Plath (1971).

The contrast between Susan and David Smith comes from Adams (1996).

The studies on linguistic style described here are well-reviewed by Pennebaker & King (1999) and by Pennebaker, Mehl, & Niederhoffer (2003). The study of people's blogs after the 9/11 attacks is Cohn, Mehl, & Pennebaker (2004) and the study of the linguistic styles of the Beatles' lyrics is Petrie, Pennebaker, & Sivertsen (2008). The manual for the LIWC is Pennebaker, Chung, Ireland, Gonzales, & Booth (2007). The concept of verbal immediacy vs. distancing was introduced by Wiener & Mehrabian (1968).

Typical experiences reported by people on LSD can be found in Johnson, Richards, & Griffiths (2008) or at http://www.emcdda.europa.eu/

publications/drug-profiles/lsd, and http://www.erowid.org/chemicals/
lsd/, and http://www.narconon.ca/LSD.htm.

See MacDonald (1994, pp. 148–153) for discussion of LSD and *Tomorrow Never Knows*.

CHAPTER 3

McAdams (1993) is among the best known psychologists who has written
about the importance of stories in human identity. Hobson (1988) proposes
a narrative approach to dreams.

The Thematic Apperception Test (TAT) was first developed by Morgan &
Murray (1935). McClelland, Atkinson, Clark, & Lowell (1953) discuss
measurement of the achievement motive via this method.

The fundamental theory behind the scripting approach is described in Demorest
& Alexander (1992) and Tomkins (1987).

The paper on the scripts of B. F. Skinner is by Demorest & Siegel (1996); the
scripts are presented on pp. 250 and 249 respectively, and are reprinted by
permission of John Wiley and Sons. The descriptions of his birthplace and
of his first experiment are from Skinner (1984, p.3) and Skinner (1956, p.
223), respectively.

The script provided by Dr. Siegel is reprinted with his permission.

For Cynthia Lennon's reflections on the difficulties in her relationship with
Lennon during this period, see, for example, pp. 181–186 of Lennon (2005).

See Alexander (1990) for the usefulness of the primacy rule.

Sheff (2000) reports Lennon's reflections regarding *Hello Little Girl* on p. 172,
and regarding *I Call Your Name* on pp. 169–170; these quotes are reprinted
by permission of St. Martin's Press.

CHAPTER 4

This dream of Freud's patient is related in slightly different forms in Freud
(1899/1999, pp. 264–265), (1920/1943, pp. 110–112) and (1952,
pp. 53–54, 58). These books also provide fine explanations of the method
of free association.

Hobson (1988) presents an overview of contemporary research into dreams.

The classic study referred to here is Meyer and Schvaneveldt (1971). Cognitive
psychologists still do not agree exactly on how concepts are organized in

people's minds, but the method applied in this chapter seems consistent
with the three major theories as described in studies by Collins & Quillian
(1969), Rips, Shoben, & Smith (1973), and Rosch & Mervis (1975).

The image of "marmalade" appears in *Alice in Wonderland* (Carroll, 2008, chapter
1, p. 10) and several other images appear in *Through the Looking Glass*,
including "looking glass" (in the title and chapter 1, pp. 127–130), a "train"
ride (chapter 3, p. 149), a "rocking-horse" (chapter 3, p. 153), and a "boat"
ride (chapter 5, p. 180, as well as in the poem that ends that book, p. 245).

The free association data set is from Nelson, McEvoy, & Schreiber (1998).

CHAPTER 5

The idea that auditory memories are organized in associative networks and can
be activated by later experiences seems well-supported by Snyder (2000).
A review of how episodic memory is associated with music can be found
in Juslin & Vastfjall (2008). The study concerning music, autobiographical
memory, and the brain is Ford, Addis, & Giovanello (2011); a similar
study was conducted by Janata (2009). Information about the storage
of procedural memories can be found in Fuster (1995), and the cases
concerning procedural musical memory in Alzheimer's patients come from
Baird & Samson (2009).

Whissel & Whissel (2000) have written an interesting article on the Beatles'
use of key.

Lennon's reflections come from Sheff (2000), pp. 174–177 for *Help!*, and
pp. 153–164 for *Strawberry Fields Forever*; they are reprinted by permission
of St. Martin's Press. Lennon's claim that these were the "only true songs" he
ever wrote is from Wenner (1971, p. 29).

CHAPTER 6

In many respects, the basic model outlined in this chapter and represented in
Figure 6.1 was influenced by the thinking of Mischel & Shoda (1995).

The chronology and details of events from Lennon's life that are reported in
all three sections of this chapter were checked across numerous sources,
including Coleman (1992), Everett (1999, 2001), Goldman (1988),
Lennon (2005), Lewisohn (1990), MacDonald (1994), Norman (2008),

and Schaffner (1978). These sources do not agree in every respect, and so I tried to take the most conservative interpretation of events and to note disagreements when they seemed relevant. If specific statements were made by particular biographers but not widely replicated across sources, I have cited them below.

Goldman (1988, pp. 29–30) claims that Julia often left Lennon alone when he was an infant.

Lennon's long quote about Julia's death and Shotton's quote about Lennon's emotional response are from Davies (1978, pp. 48–49.)

Cynthia Lennon's quote about how Lennon's family coped with Julia's death is from Lennon (2005, p. 46); it is reprinted by permission of Random House, Inc. The incident about Lennon's response to a fellow student is reported in Norman (2008, p. 153).

Attachment theory was first systematically presented by Bowlby (1969/1982, 1973, 1980) and substantially expanded and tested by Ainsworth (e.g., Ainsworth, 1964; Ainsworth, Blehar, Waters, & Wall, 1978). More recent overviews of theoretical advancements and the burgeoning empirical literature can be found in Cassidy & Shaver (1999) and Mikulincer & Shaver (2007). Some particularly useful sources for specific claims made in this section are Hazan & Shaver (1987); Kassel, Wardle, & Roberts (2007); and Weinfield, Sroufe, Egeland, & Carlson (1999).

Statements Ono and Pang made concerning Lennon's insecurity can be found, for example, in Giuliano & Giuliano (1996, pp. 168 and 214). Cynthia Lennon's perspective on his jealousy and insecurity can be found in multiple places within her 2005 book, including pp. 3, 25, 26, and 37.

Lennon's statement that he needed drugs to survive is from Wenner (1971, p. 82).

Some important theoretical work on grief and the importance of expressing one's emotions includes Freud (1917/1957), Rando (1993), Stroebe & Schut (1999), and Worden (2001). Specific findings cited here include work by Pennebaker, Zech, & Rime (2001) and Schut, Stroebe, & van den Bout (1997). General information about the ways in which people's social surroundings influence how they cope with negative emotions can be found in Cooper (1998) and Hochschild (1979).

The summary of the literature about grief and anxious-ambivalent attachment comes from Fraley & Shaver (1999, p. 742), and the study cited soon after is Fraley & Shaver (1997).

Lennon's quote about the end of touring can be found in Norman (2008, pp. 454–455).

Lennon's quotes about the effects of LSD on his ego and psyche are from Wenner (1971, pp. 40–41 and 77–78).

Reviews of the effects of LSD and LSD-based therapy can be found in Johnson, Richards, & Griffiths (2008) and Vollenweider & Kometer (2010). Less formal summaries are available at http://www.erowid.org/chemicals/lsd/, and http://www.emcdda.europa.eu/publications/drug-profiles/lsd, and http://www.narconon.ca/LSD.htm.

Lennon's response to the news of Cynthia's pregnancy, her description of their wedding, and her characterization of Lennon as "present but absent" can be found on pp. 91, 96, and 150 of Lennon (2005); quotes are reprinted by permission of Random House, Inc.

Lennon's quote regarding Julian's conception is from Sheff (2000, p. 63), and is reprinted by permission of St. Martin's Press.

Julian's drawing can be seen on the cover of his 2009 EP, *Lucy* (Lennon, 2009).

The poem that came to Lennon's mind is from Carroll (2008, p. 245).

CHAPTER 8

The vacillation described here can be understood in numerous ways. For example, Freud (1923/1960) would view it as a battle between the expressive desires of the id and the defensive strictures of the ego. Maslow (1956) would see it as a mix of the opposing motives towards growth and defense. The idea that ambivalence is fundamental to the change process is basic to the approach known as *motivational interviewing* developed and described by Miller & Rollnick (2002). Finally, these varying motives could be understood as reflective of the defensive, expressive, and restitutive functions of writing described by Elms (1994).

I undertook the same process here as described in the notes to chapter 6 regarding the events from Lennon's life that are related in this chapter. I relied in particular on Everett (1999) and MacDonald (1994) for information concerning the background on the songs described in this chapter.

Lennon's own reflections on *I Am the Walrus*, and the quote regarding Dylan, come from Sheff (2000, pp. 184–185); they are reprinted by permission of St. Martin's Press. Other biographers' suggestions about the meaning of Lennon's reference to "policemen" come from Davies (1978, p. 276) and MacDonald (1994, p. 214, footnote 2). Everett (1999, p. 133) reprints the childhood rhyme.

The séance to reach Julia's spirit is described by Goldman (1988, p. 78).

See Cassidy & Shaver (1999) or Mikulincer & Shaver (2007) for more about the pain of separation from the perspective of attachment theory.

The quote regarding *Yer Blues* is from Norman (2008, p. 534).

Lyrics of the songs are from Lowry (1988).

Quotes from Cynthia Lennon about the end of their marriage are from Lennon (2005, pp. 212–214); they are reprinted by permission of Random House, Inc.

Lennon's description of *Julia* can be found in Sheff (2000, pp. 189–190) and is reprinted by permission of St. Martin's Press. Everett (1999, pp. 170–172) and MacDonald (1994, pp. 260–261) both provide interesting analyses of this song.

Heroin's effects are well described in the *Diagnostic and Statistical Manual of Mental Disorders* (American Psychiatric Association, 2000, p. 271), on www.erowid.org/chemicals/heroin/heroin.shtml and on www.drugrehabusa.org/heroin/html. Lennon's quotes about heroin come from Goldman (1988, p. 311).

CHAPTER 9

Again, refer to the notes in chapter 6 for information on how I compiled the biographical information about Lennon's life at this time.

Janov's statements about Lennon's state at the time primal scream therapy commenced are from Norman (2008, pp. 639–640). Lennon's quotes are from Sheff (2000, p. 125, reprinted by permission of St. Martin's Press) and from an interview he did with Howard Smith of radio station WPLJ in December of 1970 (see http://homepage.ntlworld.com/carousel/pob/pob21.html).

Lyrics for the songs from the *Plastic Ono Band* album are from Lennon (1981, 1997). The "dazed child" quote is from Norman (2008, p. 652).

AFTERWORD

MacDonald (1994, p. 261) raises a similar question regarding Lennon's later creative output.

For information on how attachment beliefs can change, see Mikulincer & Shaver (2007). For evidence that old learning and beliefs persist in the face of later experiences, see Anderson, Lepper, & Ross (1980), Rescorla (1993, 1996), and Ross, Lepper, & Hubbard (1975).

NOTES ON THE METHODS

SOME GENERAL POINTS

Numerous approaches to psychobiography have influenced the multifaceted approach that I follow throughout the book. In addition to the authors who devised and articulated the specific methods used in chapters 2 through 5 (see Notes on the Text), I am especially indebted to the work of Elms (1994), McAdams (1993), Nasby & Read (1997), Runyan (1981, 1984), & Schultz (2005).

My starting point for the lyrics and music of Lennon's songs were the Hal Leonard publications of *The Complete Beatles, Volumes 1 & 2* (Lowry, 1988) and *Lennon: The Solo Years* (Lennon, 1981). When in doubt, I cross-checked the lyrics published in these books with those available on record sleeves, in *The Lyrics of John Lennon* (Lennon, 1997), and on the Internet. For analyses of the music, I also made substantial use of MacDonald's (1994) lively *Revolution in the Head: The Beatles' Records and the Sixties* and Everett's encyclopedic two-volume *The Beatles as Musicians: The Quarry Men through Rubber Soul* (2001) and *Revolver through the Anthology* (1999).

Using these sources meant that I ultimately based my analyses on the recorded versions of the songs as they appeared in their primary releases to the public. This strategy allowed for a "standardized" sample of what seems to have been the final, "endorsed" versions of the songs as Lennon wanted them to have been heard at the time (although he clearly remained dissatisfied with some of them). There are at least two main weaknesses of this strategy, however.

The first weakness concerns the issue of time. Many of the arguments in the book concern what may have been going on in Lennon's mind at the time he was writing songs, especially *Lucy in the Sky with Diamonds*. But there is no definite time point that I can know for certain corresponds to "when he was writing." Except for songs that may have sprung fully formed from Lennon's mind on the first draft, most of his songs would have undergone a process of revision; clearly that was the case for *Strawberry Fields Forever*. During the revision process, it is highly likely that Lennon's ideas about what he was trying to express and how best to express it would have shifted and evolved, with corresponding changes in the words and music that he might have used. As such, it may be that if a word was added or a key was changed rather late in his revision process, then the themes that I suggest were on Lennon's mind might not have always been so prevalent throughout his composition of the song. On the other hand, the fact that Lennon ultimately decided on the word or musical expression he did suggests that something impelled him toward that new word or musical expression, and that "something" may have been what I have proposed was on his mind.

The second weakness of this strategy concerns the influence of others on Lennon's songwriting. McCartney and Lennon collaborated deeply on many of Lennon's early songs, truly writing them together (e.g., *She Loves You*, *Little Child*). Other songs were a melding of each of their individual efforts (e.g., *A Day in the Life*). In still others, the contribution of McCartney is limited to a few images or words, but nonetheless present; such seems to be the case for *Lucy in the Sky with Diamonds* (see Spignesi & Lewis, p. 50). Later in Lennon's career, Yoko Ono also contributed to some of his songs, including *Julia*. And as the songs were rehearsed, recorded, and mixed in the studio, the other Beatles and their producer George Martin certainly made suggestions about how to improve both the lyrics and the music. For these reasons, I have omitted lyrical passages or images when information exists suggesting that such passages or images were not primarily Lennon's ideas. No doubt, however, the scientist's bane of error will have led to some mistakes in this process.

CHAPTER 2

I am particularly indebted to Cindy Chung for suggesting the comparison samples used in this chapter, as they are far more appropriate than what I was initially using in my earlier analyses. An even more representative sample of popular songs at the time would have been obtained if I had randomly selected from top-40 hits during the period, rather than just used no. 1 songs.

Some modifications were made to the lyrics of the no. 1 songs to enhance the likelihood that their words would be recognized by the LIWC dictionary. Specifically, contracted words were sometimes modified. For example, "'cuz" was changed to "because" and words like "hangin'" to "hanging."

Careful readers of Table 2.1 might note that scores for some LIWC characteristics are more extreme for the comparisons of *Lucy in the Sky with Diamonds* to no. 1 songs (in the third column) than to Lennon's other recent songs (in the second column). Examination of appendices B and C suggest that this is a joint function of *Lucy in the Sky with Diamonds'* scores on those characteristics being more similar to Lennon's average style than to the average style of no. 1 songs (not surprising) and of Lennon being more variable on those characteristics in his recent songs (i.e., having higher standard deviations) than were composers of no. 1 songs during the time period in question (somewhat surprising given the range of songwriters involved in that latter sample).

The summary immediacy score mentioned in the text was calculated by summing the z-scores for first person singular pronouns, present tense verbs, and discrepancies, and then subtracting the z-scores for articles and long words. A high score therefore represents more immediacy.

CHAPTER 3

Hello Little Girl is not included in Lowry (1988), so I obtained its lyrics from Internet sites, cross-checking them with those heard on the *Anthology I* album; lyrics for *I Call Your Name* are from Lowry (1988).

The scripting results reported here are clearly subject to interpretive biases I may have had or unconscious attempts on my part to make the resulting scripts from the earliest songs similar to the script I wrote for *Lucy in the Sky with Diamonds*. While the inclusion of Dr. Siegel's script is a step in the right direction, an even better approach would have followed the very sophisticated method used by Demorest & Siegel (1996) in their study of

B. F. Skinner to eliminate the likelihood that scriptwriting biases explained similarity between scripts.

CHAPTER 4

Baldwin (1942) influenced the methodological approach I took with Lennon's songs.

Lyrics were taken primarily from Lowry (1988). For what I hope are obvious reasons, I excluded from this concordance very common words like "to," "you," and "the." I also excluded a few words that Paul McCartney seems to have contributed to the lyrics of *Lucy in the Sky with Diamonds* (see Spignesi & Lewis, p. 50). Finally, as with the LIWC analyses, I did not search out associations to words in earlier songs where the respective contributions of Lennon and McCartney are especially difficult to disentangle (e.g., *We Can Work It Out*, *Eleanor Rigby*, *She Loves You*).

The method utilized here could have been improved if naive coders using a standardized system had rated the earlier songs that contained a word from *Lucy in the Sky with Diamonds* for the presence of particular themes (like separation or love) in the portions of the songs that contained the relevant words.

CHAPTER 5

Completion of this analysis relied primarily on the transcriptions of Lowry (1988), as well as the descriptions of the songs' musical characteristics provided by Everett (1999, 2001) and MacDonald (1994). I am indebted to Associate Professor of Music Jeremy Day-O'Connell for discussions regarding the approach taken in this chapter and for sitting down at the piano with me and helping to confirm my conclusions about the similarities between *Lucy in the Sky with Diamonds*, *Help!*, and *Strawberry Fields Forever*.

Obviously, there are other potential musical characteristics that could have served as a basis of comparison. Late in the production process of this book, I realized that among these should have been the song's tempo, i.e., the speed with which the beats unfold.

Lennon generally did not physically write out his music in the same way that Mozart or Beethoven used standardized notation to create a score. Thus, transcriptions of Lennon's music rely on subjective decisions of the listener. This made my decisions about how to code key and key change rather complicated for both *Help!* and *Strawberry Fields Forever*.

Lowry (1988) transcribes *Help!* in A major with no key changes. MacDonald (1994, p. 121) writes that *Help!* "opens on an unhappy B minor, climbing stepwise via a sixth to a pleading scream as A major arrives to stabilize the harmony." Thus, he implies both that *Help!* was written in A major and that the key changes during the song (from B minor to A major). Everett's (2001, p. 298) example transcription suggests that *Help!* was written in A major, but his discussion of the song does not explicitly mention a key change.

Strawberry Fields Forever is even more complicated. Lowry (1988) again transcribes the song in A major with no key changes. Both MacDonald (1994) and Everett (1999) describe the complicated recording process involved in creating the final version of this song, whereby portions of two different versions that had been recorded in different keys and at different tempos were electronically modified by Beatles' producer George Martin and spliced together. MacDonald (p. 174) writes that "the final mix wanders in a microtonal borderland between keys. (The track begins in an untempered A sharp before sliding imperceptibly into orthodox B flat.)" Everett (2001, pp. 78–79) provides more details, noting that an earlier take was recorded in A major and a later take was recorded "in C to sound (on replay) in B." When the two versions were merged, "Part I [of the resulting song] sounds midway between A and B flat, and Part II is much closer to B flat."

These considerations led me to conclude that it was safe to consider *Help!* and *Strawberry Fields Forever* as sharing the musical characteristic of key with *Lucy in the Sky with Diamonds*, and appendix F reflects this decision. However, I ultimately decided that it was not clear that either *Help!* or *Strawberry Fields Forever* changed key, and thus I did not count this as a shared musical characteristic. Notably, if I had counted key change as a shared characteristic, then *Help!* and *Strawberry Fields Forever* would share five, rather than four, features with *Lucy in the Sky with Diamonds*.

CHAPTER 8

As noted above, listeners often differ with regard to decisions about a song's key or potential key changes. The same can occur for potential time changes.

For example Lowry (1988) transcribed *Yer Blues* as changing from 3/4 to 4/4 time. But MacDonald wrote that the song is "a gutbucket 6/4 blues in E with a ragged additional 2/4 bar interjected for verisimilitude" (1994, pp. 245–246). And an anonymous reviewer of an earlier draft of this book stated this:

> While *Yer Blues* does shift from a very obvious 3-feel to something that might sound to a non-musician as 4/4, in reality, each of the beats of that 4/4 are still subdivided into threes. Even the section that is supposedly in 3/4 is actually organized into phrases of 4, thus 4 measures of 3/4, just as the contrasting section is in a faster meter of 4 beats of 3/8.

All three of these musical experts listened to the same recording, but they disagreed about the song's time signature(s). Given that Lennon did not provide a physical written version of the song that could reveal how he himself understood the song's meter, errors may have entered my analysis.

REFERENCES

Adams, S. H. (1996). Statement analysis: What do suspects' words really reveal? *FBI Law Enforcement Bulletin, 65, October,* 12–20.

Ainsworth, M. D. S. (1964). Patterns of attachment behavior shown by the infant in interaction with his mother. *Merrill-Palmer Quarterly, 10,* 51–58.

Ainsworth, M. D. S., Blehar, M., Waters, E., & Wall, S. (1978). *Patterns of Attachment: A Psychological Study of the Strange Situation.* Hillsdale, NJ: Erlbuam.

Alexander, I. E. (1990). *Personology: Method and Content in Personality Assessment and Psychobiography.* Durham, NC: Duke University Press.

American Psychiatric Association (2000). *Diagnostic and Statistical Manual of Mental Disorders* (4th ed., Text Revision). Washington, DC: Author.

Anderson, C. A., Lepper, M. R., & Ross, L. (1980). The perseverance of social theories: The role of explanation in the persistence of discredited information. *Journal of Personality and Social Psychology, 39,* 1037–1049.

Baird, A., & Samson, S. (2009). Memory for music in Alzheimer's disease: Unforgettable? *Neuropsychology Review, 19,* 85–101.

Baldwin, A. L. (1942). Personal structure analysis: A statistical method for investigating the single personality. *The Journal of Abnormal and Social Psychology, 37,* 163–183.

Bowlby, J. (1969/1982). *Attachment and Loss: Vol. 1. Attachment.* New York: Basic Books.

Bowlby, J. (1973). *Attachment and Loss: Vol. 2. Separation.* New York: Basic Books.

Bowlby, J. (1980). *Attachment and Loss: Vol. 3. Loss.* New York: Basic Books.

Carroll, L. (2008). *Alice's Adventures in Wonderland and Through the Looking-Glass.* New York: Oxford University Press.

Cassidy, J., & Shaver, P. R. (Eds.) (1999). *Handbook of Attachment: Theory, Research, and Clinical Applications.* New York: The Guilford Press.

Cohn, M. A., Mehl, M. R., & Pennebaker, J. W. (2004). Linguistic markers of psychological change surrounding September 11, 2001. *Psychological Science, 15,* 687–693.

Coleman, R. (1992). *Lennon: The Definitive Biography.* New York: Harper Perennial.

Collins, A. M., & Quillian, M. R. (1969). Retrieval time from semantic memory. *Journal of Verbal Learning and Verbal Behavior, 8,* 240–247.

Cooper, S. H. (1998). Changing notions of defense within psychoanalytic theory. *Journal of Personality, 66,* 947–964.

Davies, H. (1978). *The Beatles (rev. ed.).* New York: McGraw-Hill.

Demorest, A. P., & Alexander, I. E. (1992). Affective scripts as organizers of personal experience. *Journal of Personality, 60,* 645–663.

Demorest, A. P., & Siegel, P. F. (1996). Personal influences on professional work: An empirical case study of B. F. Skinner. *Journal of Personality, 64,* 243–261.

Elms, A. C. (1994). *Uncovering Lives: The Uneasy Alliance of Biography and Psychology.* New York: Oxford University Press.

Everett, W. (1999). *The Beatles as Musicians: Revolver through the Anthology.* New York: Oxford University Press.

Everett, W. (2001). *The Beatles as Musicians: The Quarry Men through Rubber Soul.* New York: Oxford University Press.

Ford, J. H., Addis, D. R., & Giovanello, K.S. (2011). Differential neural activity during search of specific and general autobiographical memories elicited by musical cues. *Neuropsychologia, 49,* 2514–2526.

Fraley, R. C., & Shaver, P. R. (1997). Adult attachment and the suppression of unwanted thoughts. *Journal of Personality & Social Psychology, 73,* 1080–1091.

Fraley, R. C., & Shaver, P. R. (1999). Loss and bereavement: Attachment theory and recent controversies concerning "grief work" and the nature of detachment. In J. Cassidy & P. R. Shaver (Eds.), *Handbook of Attachment: Theory, Research, and Clinical Applications* (pp. 735–759). New York: The Guilford Press.

Freud, S. (1899/1999). *The Interpretation of Dreams* (J. Crick, Trans.). New York: Oxford University Press.

Freud, S. (1917/1957). Mourning and melancholia. In J. Strachey (Ed. and Trans.), *Standard Edition of the Complete Psychological Works of Sigmund Freud* (Vol. 14). London: Hogarth Press.

Freud, S. (1920/1943). *A General Introduction to Psychoanalysis* (J. Riviere, Trans.). Garden City, NY: Garden City Publishing Company, Inc.

Freud, S. (1923/1960). *The Ego and the Id* (J. Strachey, Trans.). New York: W. W. Norton & Company.

Freud, S. (1952). *On Dreams* (J. Strachey, Trans.). New York: W. W. Norton & Company.

Fuster, J. M. (1995). *Memory in the Cerebral Cortex*. Cambridge, MA: MIT Press.

Giuliano, G., & Giuliano, B. (1996). *The Lost Lennon Interviews*. Holbrook, MA: Adams Media Corporation.

Goldman, A. (1988). *The Lives of John Lennon*. New York: William Morrow & Company, Inc.

Hazan, C., & Shaver, P. (1987). Romantic love conceptualized as an attachment process. *Journal of Personality & Social Psychology, 52,* 511–524.

Hobson, J. A. (1988). *The Dreaming Brain*. New York: Basic Books.

Hochschild, A. (1979). Emotion work, feeling rules, and social structure. *American Journal of Sociology, 85,* 551–575.

Janata, P. (2009). The neural architecture of music-evoked autobiographical memories. *Cerebral Cortex, 19,* 2579–2594.

Johnson, M. W., Richards, W. A., & Griffiths, R. R. (2008). Human hallucinogen research: Guidelines for safety. *Journal of Psychopharmacology, 22,* 603–620.

Juslin, P. N., & Vastfjall, D. (2008). Emotional responses to music: The need to consider underlying mechanisms. *Behavioral and Brain Sciences, 31,* 559–621.

Kassel, J. D., Wardle, M., & Roberts, J. E. (2007). Adult attachment security and college student substance abuse. *Addictive Behaviors, 32,* 1164–1176.

Lennon, C. (2005). *John*. New York: Crown Publishers.

Lennon, J. (1981). *Lennon: The Solo Years*. Milwaukee, WI: Hal Leonard Corporation.

Lennon, J. (1997). *The Lyrics of John Lennon*. London: Omnibus Press.

Lennon, J. (2009). *Lucy*. http://www.theRevolution.com

Levertov, D. (1964). *O Taste and See*. Norfolk, CT: New Directions.

Lewisohn, M. (1990). *The Beatles Day by Day: A Chronology, 1962–1989*. New York: Harmony Books.

Lowry, T. (1988). *The Complete Beatles, Volumes 1 & 2*. Milwaukee, WI: Hal Leonard Corporation.

MacDonald, I. (1994). *Revolution in the Head: The Beatles' Records and the Sixties*. New York: Henry Holt and Company.

Maslow, A. H. (1956). Defense and growth. *Merrill-Palmer Quarterly, 3,* 36–47.

McAdams, D. P. (1993). *The Stories We Live By: Personal Myths and the Making of the Self*. New York: The Guilford Press.

McClelland, D. C., Atkinson, J. W., Clark, R. A., & Lowell, E. L. (1953). *The Achievement Motive*. New York: Appleton-Century-Crofts.

Meyer, D. E., & Schvaneveldt, R. W. (1971). Facilitation in recognizing pairs of words: Evidence of a dependence between retrieval operations. *Journal of Experimental Psychology, 90,* 227–234.

Mikulincer, M., & Shaver, P. R. (2007). *Attachment in Adulthood: Structure, Dynamics, and Change*. New York: The Guilford Press.

Miller, W. R., & Rollnick, S. (2002). *Motivational Interviewing: Preparing People for Change*. New York: The Guilford Press.

Mischel, W., & Shoda, Y. (1995). A cognitive-affective system theory of personality: Reconceptualizing situations, dispositions, dynamics, and invariance in personality structure. *Psychological Review, 102,* 246–268.

Morgan, C. D., & Murray, H. A. (1935). A method for examining fantasies: The Thematic Apperception Test. *Archives of Neurology and Psychiatry, 34,* 289–306.

Nasby, W., & Read, N. W. (1997). The life voyage of a solo circumnavigator: Integrating theoretical and methodological perspectives. *Journal of Personality, 65,* 785–1068.

Nelson, D. L., McEvoy, C. L., & Schreiber, T. A. (1998). *The University of South Florida word association, rhyme, and word fragment norms.* http://w3.usf.edu/FreeAssociation/

Norman, P. (2008). *John Lennon: The Life.* New York: HarperCollins Publisher.

Pelham, B. W., Mirenberg, M. C., & Jones, J. T. (2002). Why Susie sells sea-shells by the seashore: Implicit egotism and major life decisions. *Journal of Personality and Social Psychology, 82,* 469–487.

Pennebaker, J. W., Chung, C. K., Ireland, M., Gonzales, A., & Booth, R. J. (2007). *The Development and Psychometric Properties of LIWC 2007.* Austin, TX: LIWC, Inc.

Pennebaker, J. W., & King, L. A. (1999). Linguistic styles: Language use as an individual difference. *Journal of Personality & Social Psychology, 77,* 1296–1312.

Pennebaker, J. W., Mehl, M. R., & Niederhoffer, K. G. (2003). Psychological aspects of natural language use: Our words, our selves. *Annual Review of Psychology, 54,* 547–577.

Pennebaker, J. W., & Stone, L. D. (2004). What was she trying to say? A linguistic analysis of Katie's diaries. In D. Lester (Ed.), *Katie's Diary: Unlocking the Mystery of a Suicide* (pp. 55–79). New York: Brunner-Routledge.

Pennebaker, J. W., Zech, E., & Rime, B. (2001). Disclosing and sharing emotion: Psychological, social, and health consequences. In M. S. Stroebe, R. O. Hansson, W. Stroebe, & H. Schut (Eds.), *Handbook of Bereavement Research: Consequences, Coping, and Care* (pp. 517–543). Washington, DC: American Psychological Association.

Petrie, K. J., Pennebaker, J. W., & Sivertsen, B. (2008). Things we said today: A linguistic analysis of the Beatles. *Psychology of Aesthetics, Creativity, and the Arts, 2,* 197–202.

Plath, S. (1971). *The Bell Jar.* New York: Harper & Row.

Rando, T. E. (1993). *Treatment of Complicated Mourning.* Champaign, IL: Research Press.

Rescorla, R. A. (1993). Preservation of response-outcome associations through extinction. *Animal Learning & Behavior, 21,* 238–245.

Rescorla, R. A. (1996). Spontaneous recovery after training with multiple out-comes. *Animal Learning & Behavior, 24,* 11–18.

Rips, L. J., Shoben, E. J., & Smith, E. E. (1973). Semantic distance and the verification of semantic relations. *Journal of Verbal Learning and Verbal Behavior, 12,* 1–20.

Rosch, E., & Mervis, C. B. (1975). Family resemblances: Studies in the internal structure of categories. *Cognitive Psychology, 7,* 573–605.

Ross, L., Lepper, M. R., & Hubbard, M. (1975). Perseverance in self-perception and social perception: Biased attributional processes in the debriefing paradigm. *Journal of Personality and Social Psychology, 32,* 880–892.

Runyan, W. M. (1981). Why did Van Gogh cut off his ear? The problem of alternative explanations in psychobiography. *Journal of Personality & Social Psychology, 40,* 1070–1077.

Runyan, W. M. (1984). *Life Histories and Psychobiography: Explorations in Theory and Method.* New York: Oxford University Press.

Schaffner, N. (1978). *The Beatles Forever.* New York: McGraw-Hill.

Schultz, W. T. (Ed.). (2005). *Handbook of Psychobiography.* New York: Oxford University Press.

Schut, H. A. W., Stroebe, M. S., & van den Bout, J. (1997). Intervention for the bereaved: Gender differences in the efficacy of two counseling programs. *British Journal of Clinical Psychology, 36,* 63–72.

Sheff, D. (2000). *All We Are Saying: The Last Major Interview with John Lennon and Yoko Ono.* New York: St. Martin's Griffin.

Skinner, B. F. (1956). A case history in scientific method. *American Psychologist, 11,* 221–233.

Skinner, B. F. (1984). *Particulars of My Life.* New York: New York University Press.

Snyder, B. (2000). *Music and Memory: An Introduction.* Cambridge: MIT Press.

Spignesi, S. J., & Lewis, M. (2004). *Here, There, and Everywhere: The 100 Best Beatles Songs.* New York: Black Dog & Leventhal Publishers.

Stirman, S. W., & Pennebaker, J. W. (2001). Word use in the poetry of suicidal and non-suicidal poets. *Psychosomatic Medicine, 63,* 517–522.

Stroebe, M., & Schut, H. (1999). The dual process model of coping with bereavement: Rationale and description. *Death Studies, 23,* 197–224.

Tomkins, S. S. (1987). Script theory. In J. Aronoff, A. I. Rabin, & R. Zucker (Eds.), *The Emergence of Personality* (pp. 147–216). New York: Springer.

Vollenweider, F. X., & Kometer, M. (2010). The neurobiology of psychedelic drugs: Implications for the treatment of mood disorders. *Nature Reviews: Neuroscience, 11,* 642–651.

Weinfield, N. S., Sroufe, L. A., Egeland, B., & Carlson, E. A. (1999). The nature of individual differences in infant–caregiver attachment. In J. Cassidy & P. R. Shaver (Eds.), *Handbook of Attachment: Theory, Research, and Clinical Applications* (pp. 68–88). New York: Guilford Press.

Wenner, J. S. (1971). *Lennon Remembers: The Full Rolling Stone Interviews from 1970.* New York: Popular Library.

Whissell, R., & Whissell, C. (2000). The emotional importance of key: Do Beatles' songs written in different keys convey different emotional tones? *Perceptual and Motor Skills, 91,* 973–980.

Wiener, M., & Mehrabian, A. (1968). *Language within Language: Immediacy, a Channel in Verbal Communication.* New York: Appleton-Century-Crofts.

Worden, J. W. (2001). *Children and Grief: When a Parent Dies.* New York: Guilford Press.

INDEX